40

DAYS OF
SPIRITUAL GROWTH

MANNY RIVERA

Cover Design: Cheyanna Rose Pelham

Print ISBN: 979-8-9923412-3-2
Library of Congress Control Number: 2025901912

Table of Contents

Foreword

I am not a "devotional" person. Long ago, when I set out on a journey to read and study the Bible, I decided that I had too long used the devotions and Bible studies designed to help me as a crutch. This is not, however, a book that will allow itself to be a crutch for anyone. This is a devotional that will implore you and encourage you to go deeper on your faith journey. Pastor Manny Rivera's insights are a tool to help reveal areas in your walk with Christ that need challenging, refining, and strengthening.

When I first met Manny Rivera I was 34 years old. With a passion for Jesus and a newfound interest in Bible study, I was more than a little wet behind the ears. I did not know the word of God inside and out, and I knew very little about applying what I did know. I had been a Christian most of my life, but I lacked understanding. I was trying, as best as I could, to be found faithful. However, I had many beliefs and habits that did not align with scripture. Through many challenging teachings, conversations and the revealing of the word, Manny Rivera encouraged me to be the woman I am today.

Nearly eight years later I am by no means perfect, but I am more well-versed in the Bible in general, hermeneutics (that's how you interpret scripture for all you non-theologian types), and aligning my life with its principles. I know beyond a shadow of a doubt that I have been created with a purpose and that whatever the Lord has purposed for me, He has provision and empowerment for that purpose. You have purpose, provision, and empowerment for that purpose as well. It will not come without trials, but this book reminds us that God will use any and everything in our lives to grow us. It will not all be easy, it will not all be fun, but it will be worth it.

I believe that if you allow this book and its words to challenge your thought patterns and drive you towards the further study of scripture, praying for God to reveal to you your own heart, you will forever be changed.

1 Corinthians 1:18 says "For the word of the cross is folly to those who are perishing, but to us who are being saved it is the power of God." We have to believe that the word for us is the power of God. To truly believe that is to live it out. And it will transform our lives, our marriages, our

dysfunctions, and our homes. In order to see this realized, we have to ingest and digest the Word of God, rightly applying it in our lives. Pastor Manny Rivera's 40 Days to Spiritual Growth will challenge you to do just that. Not to let scripture and its principles just be words on a page, but to allow the word to do what Hebrews 4:12 calls "piercing to the division of soul and of spirit." I hope you enjoy the journey!

With Gratitude,

Andrea McMahon
Executive Pastor of Discover Life Church
Lawrenceville, GA
www.AndreaMcMahonWrites.com

Dedication

I dedicate this book to my children, Calysta, Zayne, Zion, Erika and Zealynd. May you continue to grow in the faith and knowledge of our Lord Jesus Christ.

Introduction

Embrace the Journey of Spiritual Growth

Welcome to 40 Days of Spiritual Growth, a journey designed to lead you into a deeper relationship with God, unlock your true potential, and transform your life from the inside out. This book is not just another devotional; it's a roadmap to spiritual maturity, guiding you through the daily challenges and triumphs of living a life fully committed to Christ.

We live in a world that constantly pulls us in different directions, with distractions at every turn. It's easy to lose sight of what truly matters and allow our spiritual lives to take a back seat. But deep down, we know that there's more to life than just getting by. We crave a deeper connection with God, a sense of purpose that goes beyond the mundane, and the strength to overcome the challenges we face. This book is your invitation to step out of the ordinary and embark on a journey that will change your life.

Each day of this 40-day journey is crafted to help you grow in your faith, challenge your thinking, and inspire you to live out your calling with passion and purpose. From understanding the importance of commitment to exploring the power of unity, each entry is designed to meet you where you are and take you to a new level of spiritual depth. You'll discover how to navigate life's challenges, how to cultivate a heart of worship, and how to live with integrity in a world that often values convenience over conviction.

But this journey is not just about gaining knowledge; it's about transformation. As you engage with each entry, you'll find practical steps to apply the principles you learn to your daily life. You'll be encouraged to take action, to step out in faith, and to trust God in ways you never have before. The goal is not just to fill your mind with information but to ignite your heart with a passion for God that will fuel your spiritual growth long after these 40 days are over.

One of the key themes woven throughout this book is the power of consistency. Spiritual growth doesn't happen overnight; it's the result of daily choices and persistent effort. You'll be challenged to develop new habits, to break free from old patterns, and to commit to the process of becoming the person God created you to be. As you do, you'll begin to see the fruit of your labor—a deeper relationship with God, a stronger faith, and a life that reflects His glory.

As you read through 40 Days of Spiritual Growth, expect to be inspired, expect to be challenged, and expect to be changed. This is not just another book; it's a tool for transformation. Whether you're new to the faith or have been walking with God for years, this journey is for you. It's a journey that will stretch you, grow you, and ultimately bring you closer to the heart of God.

So, are you ready to embark on this journey? Are you ready to discover what God has in store for you over the next 40 days? Let's dive in together with open hearts and expectant spirits, ready to see God do something extraordinary in our lives. Your journey to spiritual growth begins now.

Why 40 Days?

Numbers in the Bible often carry profound spiritual and symbolic significance, offering insights into God's character and His plans for humanity. Throughout Scripture, numbers like 21, 40, and 52 appear in key narratives, each with its unique meaning and purpose. The number 21 can symbolize a time of expectation, completion, and perfection, as seen in the 21-day period of Daniel's fasting and prayer (Daniel 10:2-3) that led to divine revelation. The number 40 is frequently associated with periods of testing, trial, and transformation, signifying a time of spiritual preparation and renewal. Meanwhile, the number 52 can symbolize restoration and unity, as demonstrated by Nehemiah's rebuilding of Jerusalem's walls in 52 days (Nehemiah 6:15). These numbers collectively emphasize the importance of God's timing and purpose, guiding us through times of challenge and renewal toward divine fulfillment.

Biblical and Spiritual Insights

In the Bible, the number 40 is often associated with periods of trial and testing that lead to spiritual growth and preparation for new beginnings. Here are some key examples:

1. The Flood: God caused it to rain for 40 days and 40 nights during the time of Noah (Genesis 7:12). This period was a time of judgment and cleansing for the earth, leading to a new beginning for humanity through Noah's family.

2. Moses on Mount Sinai: Moses spent 40 days and nights on Mount Sinai receiving the Law from God (Exodus 24:18). This period of divine revelation and instruction prepared the Israelites for their covenant relationship with God.

3. The Israelites' Wilderness Journey: The Israelites wandered in the wilderness for 40 years (Numbers 14:33-34). This period was a time of testing and dependence on God, preparing them to enter the Promised Land.

4. Jesus' Temptation: Jesus fasted for 40 days and nights in the wilderness, where He was tempted by Satan (Matthew 4:1-2). This period of testing strengthened Him for His public ministry.

5.   **The Resurrection to Ascension**: After His resurrection, Jesus appeared to His disciples over 40 days before ascending to heaven (Acts 1:3). This period was a time of instruction and preparation for the disciples to carry out their mission.

Inspirational and Prophetic Application

The number 40 can be seen as a symbol of transformation and preparation, encouraging individuals to embrace periods of testing and growth. Here are some ways the significance of the number 40 can be applied to our lives:

1.   **Endurance and Perseverance**: The number 40 reminds us that periods of trial and testing are part of the spiritual journey. Like the Israelites in the wilderness or Jesus in the desert, we are called to endure and persevere through challenging times, trusting in God's provision and strength.

2.   **Spiritual Preparation:** Just as Moses and Jesus used their 40-day periods for spiritual preparation, we can use times of trial to deepen our relationship with God and prepare for the next season of life. This may involve prayer, fasting, and seeking God's guidance and wisdom.

3.   **Renewal and Transformation:** The number 40 signifies a time of renewal and transformation, where old patterns and behaviors are shed, and new growth occurs. We are invited to embrace change and allow God to transform us from the inside out, leading to greater spiritual maturity and purpose.

4.   **Trust in God's Timing:** The 40-day or 40-year periods in the Bible highlight the importance of trusting in God's timing. We are reminded that God is working in our lives, even when the journey seems long and arduous. By trusting in His plan, we can rest assured that He is leading us toward His intended purpose.

5.   **Prophetic Vision and Mission:** Embracing the prophetic meaning of the number 40 encourages us to seek God's vision for our lives. It invites us to align our goals and actions with His divine purpose, stepping into the roles and responsibilities He has prepared for

us. By living with intentionality and purpose, we can make a meaningful impact in our world.

The number 40 carries a deep spiritual significance that inspires us to embrace
periods of testing, transformation, and renewal. Whether applied to personal
growth or communal efforts, it serves as a reminder of God's faithfulness and
the transformative power of His grace. As we embark on a 40-day journey of
devotion and teaching, let us embrace the prophetic significance of this number,
allowing it to guide us into a deeper relationship with God and a more purposeful life.

Day 1:

Say Goodbye to Inverted Christianity

In our spiritual journey, it is crucial to recognize the dangers of what can be termed "inverted Christianity." This mindset suggests that following Christ is primarily about making our lives easier, steering away from challenges, and seeking comfort above all else. However, the true call of Christianity is to embrace the challenges of life as opportunities for growth, progress, and fulfillment of God's purpose. By saying goodbye to inverted Christianity, we can live a life of adventure and impact, fully embracing the challenges that come our way.

The Nature of Challenges

Embracing Resistance

Our life can only progress as far as our next challenge. Challenges are not obstacles to be avoided but rather opportunities for growth and progress. The human psyche often desires the road of least resistance, yet we were not fashioned by our Creator to flee from challenges. Instead, God designed us to be productive and to work through resistance to achieve dominion and purpose.

Genesis 1:28 (NIV) states, "God blessed them and said to them, 'Be fruitful and increase in number; fill the earth and subdue it. Rule over the fish in the sea and the birds in the sky and over every living creature that moves on the ground.'"

God's command to Adam and Eve to have dominion implies that challenges are inherent in our design. Dominion cannot be achieved without facing resistance and overcoming obstacles.

The Desire for Ease

Despite our design for productivity and dominion, there is a natural inclination to seek ease and avoid challenges. Our society is geared toward making life as undemanding as possible. Many small businesses are service-based, designed to make life easier by taking care of tasks such as car maintenance, cleaning, and repairs. While these services are not inherently wrong, the danger arises when the desire for ease becomes the aspiration of our Christian walk.

Philippians 4:13 (NIV) reminds us, "I can do all this through him who gives me strength."

The strength to overcome challenges and grow spiritually is found in Christ, not in avoiding difficulties. Embracing challenges as opportunities to rely on God's strength leads to spiritual growth and maturity.

The Pitfalls of Inverted Christianity

Self-Centered Faith

Inverted Christianity centers on the belief that Christ came to make life easier. It suggests that following Jesus means avoiding resistance, challenges, and problems. This mindset is self-centered, focusing on self-preservation rather than impacting the community and fulfilling God's purpose.

Matthew 16:24 (NIV) instructs, "Then Jesus said to his disciples, 'Whoever wants to be my disciple must deny themselves and take up their cross and follow me.'"

True discipleship involves self-denial and embracing the challenges that come with following Christ. It is not about seeking personal comfort but about living for a higher purpose.

A Life Without Growth

Inverted Christianity leads to a life devoid of growth, increase, and development. By avoiding challenges, we miss out on the opportunities for transformation and maturity that God provides. The Holy Spirit is not invited to follow us; rather, we are called to follow Him into the adventure of faith.

James 1:2-4 (NIV) encourages us, "Consider it pure joy, my brothers and sisters, whenever you face trials of many kinds, because you know that the testing of your faith produces perseverance. Let perseverance finish its work so that you may be mature and complete, not lacking anything."

Trials and challenges are essential for developing perseverance and maturity. By embracing these experiences, we grow in faith and become more effective instruments of God's love and grace.

Embracing the Adventure of Faith

Following the Spirit

We have been provoked to follow Him. My prayer is that everyone in our church would realize that life is designed to be an adventure. By embracing the cause of Christ, we live with the purpose of making a difference in the lives of others. This involves facing persecution, challenges, and resistance in preaching the Gospel and serving our communities.

Acts 1:8 (NIV) promises, "But you will receive power when the Holy Spirit comes on you; and you will be my witnesses in Jerusalem, and in all Judea and Samaria, and to the ends of the earth."

The power of the Holy Spirit equips us to face challenges and fulfill our mission. As we follow His leading, we say goodbye to inverted Christianity and embrace a life of growth, increase, and purpose.

The Call to Impact

As we engage in this devotional, it will shape us into people willing to face the challenges of preaching the Gospel in our communities. As we follow the Spirit's lead, we will experience transformation and impact.

2 Timothy 1:7 (NIV) assures us, "For the Spirit God gave us does not make us timid, but gives us power, love, and self-discipline."

God has given us the power, love, and discipline to overcome challenges and make a meaningful impact. By embracing the adventure of faith, we become agents of change and transformation in the world.

Application

Reflect on your current mindset and approach to challenges. Are you embracing the adventure of faith, or have you fallen into the trap of inverted Christianity? Consider how you can shift your perspective to see challenges as opportunities for growth and impact.

Spend time in prayer, asking God to reveal any areas where you have sought ease and comfort over His purpose. Seek His guidance in embracing the challenges of faith and following the leading of the Holy Spirit.

Challenge Questions

1.   How can you shift your mindset from seeking ease and comfort to embracing the challenges of faith?

2.   In what ways can you follow the leading of the Holy Spirit and impact your community with the Gospel?

3.   Reflect on a time when you faced a significant challenge in your spiritual journey. How did that experience contribute to your growth and maturity?

By saying goodbye to inverted Christianity and embracing the adventure of faith, we align ourselves with God's purpose and experience the fullness of His work in our lives. Trust in God's strength and guidance, and step boldly into the challenges and opportunities He has prepared for you.

Day 2:

It's About the Company You Keep

Our relationships significantly shape the direction and quality of our lives. Whether we realize it or not, everything that comes into our lives does so through relationships—be they beneficial or detrimental. Scripture tells us, "Bad company corrupts good morals" (1 Corinthians 15:33, NIV). This truth highlights the power and influence of those we surround ourselves with. If bad company can lead us astray, then it follows that good company can elevate us, fostering integrity and character. With integrity and character in our corner, we position ourselves for God's favor. Truly, it's about the company you keep.

The Influence of Relationships

Learning from Bishop Tony Miller

This principle was taught to me years ago by my pastor, Bishop Tony Miller. As I watched him grow in his ministry, I observed how guarded he was with the relationships he cultivated. Today, he stands as a testament to the power of intentional relationships. Bishop Miller's success and growth in ministry can be attributed largely to the company he kept. He surrounded himself with people who challenged him, held him accountable, and supported his vision.

Proverbs 13:20 (NIV) states, "Walk with the wise and become wise, for a companion of fools suffers harm."

The wisdom and character of those around us can profoundly impact our journey, encouraging us to pursue God's purpose with clarity and conviction.

The Impact on Our Development

Who we are today is because of the people in our lives. We develop as believers through the relationships we form and nurture. These relationships speak volumes about who we are and who we are becoming. In the churches we pastor and oversee, we continue to emphasize the importance of surrounding ourselves with the right people. The product of our lives derives from the company we keep. It is imperative that we develop relationships that improve us on every level.

Ecclesiastes 4:9-10 (NIV) reminds us, "Two are better than one, because they have a good return for their labor: If either of them falls down, one can help the other up. But pity anyone who falls and has no one to help them up."

Relationships provide support, encouragement, and accountability, enabling us to grow and thrive in our spiritual walk.

Receiving and Giving

We need people above us—fathers, mothers, spiritual mentors—who can pour into our lives and keep us in check. These individuals provide guidance, wisdom, and correction, helping us navigate life's challenges and stay aligned with God's purpose.

2 Timothy 2:2 (NIV) emphasizes the importance of passing on what we have learned: "And the things you have heard me say in the presence of many witnesses entrust to reliable people who will also be qualified to teach others."

Mentors and spiritual leaders equip us to grow in our faith and, in turn, enable us to pour into others, sharing the wisdom and insight we have received.

Building Peer Relationships

In addition to those who mentor us, we also need peers—friends we can hang out with, dream with, and grow alongside. These relationships offer companionship, mutual support, and shared vision. They encourage us to pursue our goals and dreams, holding us accountable to our commitments.

Proverbs 17:17 (NIV) states, "A friend loves at all times, and a brother is born for a time of adversity."

Our peers walk alongside us in both joy and adversity, providing a support system that strengthens us through life's ups and downs.

The Anointing Flows from Relationships

Nurturing Our Relationship with God

The ultimate relationship we must nurture is our relationship with God. The essence of God's activity in us flows from this relationship, as well as from our relationships with others. Our connection with God is the source of our strength, wisdom, and anointing. It is through this relationship that we are equipped to fulfill our purpose and make a meaningful impact in the world.

John 15:5 (NIV) declares, "I am the vine; you are the branches. If you remain in me and I in you, you will bear much fruit; apart from me you can do nothing."

Our relationship with God is the foundation upon which all other relationships are built. It is the conduit through which His love, grace, and power flow into our lives and the lives of those around us.

Passion for God and People

The anointing flows from a passion for God and a passion for people. As we cultivate a deep, abiding relationship with God, His love and power are poured into us, enabling us to impact others. This anointing requires a conduit, and that conduit is our relationship with God and our commitment to loving and serving others.

Matthew 22:37-39 (NIV) summarizes the greatest commandments: "Jesus replied: 'Love the Lord your God with all your heart and with all your soul and with all your mind.' This is the first and greatest commandment. And the second is like it: 'Love your neighbor as yourself.'"

By prioritizing our relationship with God and extending His love to others, we become vessels through which His anointing flows, bringing transformation and healing to those we encounter.

Application

Reflect on the relationships in your life. Are they drawing you closer to God and encouraging you to grow, or are they leading you away from His purposes? Consider how you can cultivate relationships that align with God's will and contribute to your spiritual development.

Spend time in prayer, asking God to reveal any relationships that need adjustment and to guide you in building connections that honor Him. Seek His wisdom in nurturing your relationship with Him and with others.

Challenge Questions

1.   How can you cultivate relationships that enhance your spiritual growth and align with God's purposes for your life?

2.   In what ways can you prioritize your relationship with God, allowing His love and anointing to flow through you to others?

3.   Reflect on a relationship that has significantly impacted your spiritual journey. How can you continue to nurture that connection and extend its influence to others?

By recognizing the importance of the company we keep, we can build relationships that reflect God's love and purpose, fostering growth and transformation in our lives and the lives of those around us. Embrace the power of relationships, and allow God's anointing to flow through you as you impact the world for His glory.

Day 3:

Embracing True Transition

Transition seems to have become a buzzword in the church today. We hear it all the time: transitioning from places, responsibilities, friendships, and more. At times, it irritates me how people use it as an excuse. They make permanent decisions based on temporary circumstances and call it "transition." Whatever happened to faithfulness? What happened to consistency? What about forgiveness and walking through the process of relationships? Here's the clincher: Whatever happened to faithfulness?

The Nature of Transition

Transition is an inherent part of life. Every day, we transition in one way or another. As we grow older, we transition. As we grow in Christ, we transition. As we study and learn, we transition. Transition is a natural part of our journey. So, why is something so commonly used as the reason why we, as a church, cannot remain constant, consistent, and faithful to the call of God?

We live in a migratory generation, inconsistent and unstable, unable to remain faithful to a certain location or people. We often use the term "transition" to justify our inability to stay on the path to our destiny. But true transition is not about abandoning our commitments or relationships; it's about growth, transformation, and remaining faithful to God's purpose for our lives.

Embracing Faithfulness

In a world where change is constant, faithfulness is a rare virtue. It requires commitment, perseverance, and a steadfast focus on God's calling. The Bible repeatedly emphasizes the importance of faithfulness in our journey.

Proverbs 3:3-4 (NIV) says, *"Let love and faithfulness never leave you; bind them around your neck, write them on the tablet of your heart. Then you will win favor and a good name in the sight of God and man."*

Faithfulness involves maintaining a steadfast dedication to our relationships, responsibilities, and spiritual growth. It means staying true to our commitments, even when circumstances are challenging or inconvenient.

The Call to Consistency

Consistency is closely linked to faithfulness. It is the ability to remain steadfast and reliable in our actions, words, and commitments. In our journey with Christ, consistency is crucial for spiritual growth and maturity. Galatians 6:9 (NIV) encourages us, "Let us not become weary in doing good, for at the proper time we will reap a harvest if we do not give up."

Consistency involves showing up, even when it's difficult. It means persevering through challenges and remaining faithful to God's call. By cultivating consistency, we demonstrate our trust in God's plan and our willingness to walk the path He has set before us.

The Misuse of Transition

In the church, the concept of transition is often misused to justify abandoning commitments or relationships. People may claim they are in a season of transition to avoid dealing with the complexities and challenges of life. However, using transition as an excuse can lead to instability and hinder our spiritual growth.

True transition should be rooted in a desire for growth and alignment with God's purpose. It should not be an excuse for avoiding difficult conversations or abandoning commitments. Instead, it should be a reflection of our willingness to embrace change while remaining faithful to God and His calling.

Navigating Challenges with Faithfulness

Life presents us with challenges and opportunities for growth. How we respond to these challenges determines our spiritual maturity and ability to navigate transitions effectively. By choosing faithfulness and consistency, we position ourselves to overcome obstacles and embrace God's transformative work in our lives. James 1:2-4 (NIV) reminds us, "Consider it pure joy, my brothers and sisters, whenever you face trials of many kinds, because you know that the testing of your faith produces perseverance. Let perseverance finish its work so that you may be mature and complete, not lacking anything."

Through challenges, God refines our character and strengthens our faith. By remaining faithful and consistent, we demonstrate our trust in His ability to guide us through every season of life.

Seeking God's Guidance

In moments of transition, it is essential to seek God's guidance and wisdom. Rather than making impulsive decisions based on temporary emotions, we should seek His will and direction. Prayer and discernment play a vital role in navigating transitions with faithfulness and integrity. **Proverbs 3:5-6** (NIV) advises, "Trust in the Lord with all your heart and lean not on your own understanding; in all your ways submit to him, and he will make your paths straight."

By seeking God's guidance, we align ourselves with His purpose and gain clarity on the path forward. Trusting in His wisdom allows us to navigate transitions with confidence and grace.

Embracing True Transition

True transition involves growth, transformation, and alignment with God's will. It is not about avoiding challenges or abandoning commitments; it's about embracing the opportunities for spiritual growth and development. By cultivating faithfulness, consistency, and a reliance on God's guidance, we can navigate transitions effectively and fulfill our God-given purpose.

The Role of Forgiveness

In our relationships and transitions, forgiveness plays a crucial role. It is essential to let go of past hurts and grievances to move forward with grace and love. Forgiveness allows us to release bitterness and resentment, creating space for healing and reconciliation. Colossians 3:13 (NIV) instructs us, "Bear with each other and forgive one another if any of you has a grievance against someone. Forgive as the Lord forgave you."

By embracing forgiveness, we demonstrate Christ's love and reflect His character in our interactions with others. It enables us to build healthy relationships and fosters an environment of growth and unity.

Application

Reflect on the areas in your life where you may have used transition as an excuse for avoiding commitments or challenges. Consider how you can cultivate faithfulness, consistency, and forgiveness in your relationships and spiritual journey.

Spend time in prayer, asking God to reveal areas in your life where you need to embrace true transition. Seek His guidance in navigating challenges and opportunities for growth.

Challenge Questions

1.   How can you cultivate faithfulness and consistency in your relationships and spiritual journey?

2.   In what ways can you seek God's guidance and wisdom during times of transition and change?

3.   Reflect on a past transition that was challenging. How did you respond, and what lessons can you apply moving forward?

By embracing true transition and remaining faithful to God's calling, we can navigate life's challenges with grace and purpose. Trust in His guidance, cultivate faithfulness, and embrace the transformative work He is doing in your life. Transition is not an excuse for avoiding growth; it is an opportunity to align with God's will and fulfill His purpose for your life.

Day 4:

The Transformative Power of Studying God's Word

Studying God's Word has been and will continue to be the foundation for defining who I am and what I am purposed to be. Over the years, I have realized that studying His Word is not simply about reading a book like a magazine or novel. While I can speed-read through various types of material, the Bible requires a different approach. It demands time, reflection, and a systematic process to uncover its depth and significance. This journey has taught me invaluable lessons about engaging with Scripture, seeking God's guidance, and allowing His Word to shape my life.

Approaching the Bible with Prayer

The journey of studying God's Word begins with prayer. Before I open the Bible, I pray and ask the Lord to reveal things I have not seen before. This prayerful approach acknowledges that the Word of God is supernatural, with an unfathomable depth that transcends time and culture. It has stood the test of time and remains eternally relevant. Through prayer, I invite the Holy Spirit to illuminate the Scriptures, providing insight and understanding beyond my natural comprehension. Psalm 119:18 (NIV) reminds us, "Open my eyes that I may see wonderful things in your law."

By inviting God into the study of His Word, we position ourselves to receive revelation and wisdom that transforms our hearts and minds.

The Systematic Study of Scripture

Studying the Bible is a systematic process that involves careful observation and reflection. As I read, I look out for four key elements: principles, patterns, people, and prophetic parallels. These elements provide a framework for understanding the depth and richness of God's Word.

1. Principles

Principles are fundamental truths, laws, or methods of operation that provide answers and explain God's truths in ways we can understand. They are the foundational building blocks of Scripture, offering guidance for living a life aligned with God's will.

For example, the principle of sowing and reaping in Galatians 6:7-9 (NIV) teaches us about the consequences of our actions and the importance of perseverance: "Do not be deceived: God cannot be mocked. A man reaps what he sows. Whoever sows to please their flesh, from the flesh will reap destruction; whoever sows to please the Spirit, from the Spirit will reap eternal life. Let us not become weary in doing good, for at the proper time we will reap a harvest if we do not give up."

Identifying principles within Scripture allows us to apply God's wisdom to our daily lives, guiding our decisions and shaping our character.

2. Patterns

As we read the Bible, we notice that it is full of principles. When these principles are compared to others in different books of the Bible, patterns emerge. Patterns are repetitive principles that demonstrate God's consistent relationship with humanity.

For example, the pattern of Israel's hot and cold relationship with God is evident in the book of Judges and 2 Chronicles. This pattern reflects how we, at times, live out our relationship with God—oscillating between faithfulness and disobedience.

Judges 2:18-19 (NIV) illustrates this cycle: "Whenever the Lord raised up a judge for them, he was with the judge and saved them out of the hands of their enemies as long as the judge lived; for the Lord relented because of their groaning under those who oppressed and afflicted them. But when the judge died, the people returned to ways even more corrupt than those of their ancestors, following other gods and serving and worshiping them. They refused to give up their evil practices and stubborn ways."

Recognizing patterns helps us understand God's character and the ways He interacts with His people, providing insight into our spiritual journey.

3. People

Studying the lives of men and women in the Bible offers practical lessons in God's guidance. The principles and patterns derived from their experiences, choices, victories, and failures provide invaluable nuggets of truth and wisdom.

For instance, the life of David paints a vivid picture of a journey to destiny. His story teaches us about courage, repentance, and reliance on God's strength.

1 Samuel 17:45-47 (NIV) captures David's faith as he faces Goliath: "David said to the Philistine, 'You come against me with sword and spear and javelin, but I come against you in the name of the Lord Almighty, the God of the armies of Israel, whom you have defied. This day the Lord will deliver you into my hands, and I'll strike you down and cut off your head.'"

Additionally, Abraham's life exemplifies a life of faith, patience, and promise. His journey of trust in God's promises encourages us to walk by faith, even when circumstances seem uncertain. Hebrews 11:8-10 (NIV) highlights Abraham's faith: "By faith Abraham, when called to go to a place he would later receive as his inheritance, obeyed and went, even though he did not know where he was going."

Studying the lives of biblical figures provides practical examples of living out faith in everyday situations.

4. Prophetic Parallels

Once we engage with the Word and recognize principles, patterns, and people, we begin to discern prophetic parallels. These moments occur when the Word jumps out at us, guiding our lives and offering direction, confirmation, and wisdom.

Prophetic parallels occur when God's Word speaks directly to our current circumstances, providing clarity and insight. It's as if the Scriptures come alive, offering guidance and revelation for our specific situations. Psalm 119:105 (NIV) affirms the guiding nature of God's Word: "Your word is a lamp for my feet, a light on my path."

Engaging with the Bible in this way allows us to hear God's voice, offering guidance and direction for our lives.

Application

Studying God's Word is a dynamic process that requires intentionality, prayer, and reflection. By identifying principles, patterns, people, and prophetic parallels, we uncover the richness and depth of Scripture, allowing God's truth to transform our lives.

Challenge Questions:

1.   How can you incorporate prayer and intentional reflection into your study of God's Word?

2.   In what ways can you identify principles, patterns, people, and prophetic parallels as you engage with Scripture?

3.   Reflect on a time when God's Word provided clarity and direction in your life. How can you continue to seek His guidance through Scripture?

By embracing a systematic approach to studying God's Word, we open ourselves to His transformative work, allowing His truth to shape our hearts and minds. Let the Word of God be your guide, offering wisdom, direction, and encouragement for every step of your journey.

Day 5:

Adding Value to People

One day during my morning reading, I came across the phrase "adding value to people," and it caught my attention. As I reflected on this concept, I realized that this quality is something I need to develop more in my life. Adding value is not simply about encouraging others, which I feel I do well. Instead, it involves placing trust in people to take on responsibilities and supporting them through the process until the task is completed. It means believing in them, even when others may not.

I have a tendency to be a micromanager. While I have improved tremendously over the years and have empowered many leaders who are actively working in our ministry, the Holy Spirit challenged me to have a deeper understanding of adding value to people.

The Example of Barnabas

In my study of the book of Acts, I revisited the life and ministry of Barnabas. He was a true encourager and a lifter of people. He seized every opportunity to add value to others, and without his influence, the Apostle Paul might not have received acceptance and endorsement from the founding apostles. Barnabas's willingness to invest in others significantly impacted the early church and its leadership.

What Barnabas Did

Barnabas exemplified what it means to add value to others through the following actions:

1. **Seeing Potential**: Barnabas saw the potential in Paul that no one else did. Despite Paul's past as a persecutor of Christians, Barnabas believed in the transformative work of Christ within him.

2. **Looking Beyond Mistakes**: Barnabas looked past Paul's previous mistakes and recognized the call of God on his life. He believed

in the Christ inside of Paul, despite his past transgressions.

3. Certifying Call and Leadership: Barnabas certified Paul's call and leadership to other leaders, giving him the opportunity to grow in his ministry.

4. Empowering Potential: Barnabas empowered Paul's potential by providing opportunities and support, allowing Paul to fulfill his calling.

These actions illustrate the true essence of adding value: recognizing and nurturing potential in others, even when it is not immediately apparent.

Overcoming Hesitation to Endorse Others

Many of us are hesitant to believe in and endorse individuals who have not yet proven themselves. We often protect our reputations, waiting for approval from others before offering our own support. This caution can prevent us from recognizing and nurturing potential in others. I understand the longing to be recognized and accepted in certain circles and have often prayed for God to open doors. He frequently sends a "Barnabas" to open that door for us.

The Price of Adding Value

Sometimes, the quality of adding value to others can come at a significant price. Barnabas's relationship with John Mark exemplifies this. John Mark failed miserably on a missionary journey with Paul and Barnabas, abandoning them in the process. Paul was reluctant to allow John Mark to rejoin them, but Barnabas believed in giving him a second chance and continued to invest in him.

This disagreement led to the separation of Paul and Barnabas. However, over time, the situation was resolved, and John Mark became a valuable asset to Paul's ministry. Barnabas's willingness to add value to John Mark, even at the risk of conflict, ultimately contributed to John Mark's growth and development. 2 Timothy 4:11 (NIV) highlights this transformation: "Get Mark and bring him with you, because he is helpful to me in my ministry."

Gratitude for Those Who Add Value

I am deeply thankful for the people who have added value to me throughout my life. They saw my potential before any tangible fruit was evident and took risks by putting their reputations on the line for my sake, even when I made mistakes. Their belief in me has been instrumental in my growth and development, and I am forever grateful for their investment in my life. Proverbs 27:17 (NIV) reminds us, "As iron sharpens iron, so one person sharpens another." The people who add value to our lives play a critical role in shaping us and helping us grow.

A Prayer for Discernment and Opportunity

As a leader in our network and the lead pastor of our church, I am committed to learning how to see through the dirt in people's lives and find the gold within them. I pray for discernment and the ability to notice the potential in others, just as Barnabas did with Paul. James 1:5 (NIV) encourages us to seek wisdom from God: "If any of you lacks wisdom, you should ask God, who gives generously to all without finding fault, and it will be given to you."

Empowering the "Pauls" in Our Lives

My prayer is for opportunities to empower and add value to the "Pauls" in our midst—those individuals with great potential who may need someone to believe in them and open doors for their growth.

Practical Steps for Adding Value

To actively add value to others, we can take several practical steps:

1. **Identify Potential:** Be on the lookout for individuals with potential, even if it is not immediately evident. Pay attention to their unique gifts and talents.

2. **Offer Encouragement:** Provide genuine encouragement and support, affirming their strengths and abilities. Encourage them to pursue their passions and callings.

3. **Provide Opportunities:** Create opportunities for growth and development, allowing individuals to step into new roles and responsibilities.

4. **Mentor and Guide**: Offer mentorship and guidance, walking alongside them as they navigate challenges and pursue their goals.

5. Celebrate Achievements: Celebrate their successes and milestones, recognizing their hard work and dedication.

6. Be Patient and Forgiving: Be patient with their growth process and forgiving of mistakes. Offer second chances and continue to believe in their potential.

By taking these steps, we can create an environment where individuals feel valued, empowered, and encouraged to reach their full potential.

Challenge Questions

1.   How can you become more intentional about recognizing and nurturing the potential in others?

2.   In what ways can you provide opportunities for growth and development within your community or organization?

3.   Reflect on a time when someone added value to your life. How did their investment impact you, and how can you pay it forward?

Adding value to others is a transformative process that requires intentionality, patience, and a willingness to invest in the potential of those around us. By following the example of Barnabas and seeking opportunities to empower and support others, we can create a culture of growth, encouragement, and mutual respect. Let us commit to being people who add value to others, trusting that our efforts will lead to a flourishing community where everyone is empowered to fulfill their God-given potential.

Day 6

Who's in Charge?

Back in the 80s, there was a sitcom titled Charles in Charge featuring Scott Baio as a college-age student hired as a live-in babysitter in exchange for room and board. Like many sitcoms, it didn't have an ongoing plot or significant purpose. As a teenager watching the show, one thing stood out to me: despite the title, Charles was never really in charge. This is a reflection of a deeper issue that has been present since the beginning of time—the struggle over who's in charge.

The Universal Power Struggle

The question of "who's in charge" lies at the heart of most conflicts on Earth. Whether in our personal lives or our spiritual journey with God, there is an ongoing power struggle about authority and control. This struggle manifests in various arenas and levels of life:

- **In Relationships:** Men and women often wrestle over control and influence within relationships, striving to establish dominance or equality.

- **In Families:** Children and parents may struggle over who has authority in the home. Siblings fight over territory, possessions, and countless other issues.

- **In Society:** Political parties compete for power, sports teams battle for dominance, and nations vie against nations for global influence.

The "who's in charge" question is a fundamental issue that impacts all aspects of life. It's a conflict that has existed since the dawn of time, rooted in humanity's desire for power and control.

Reflecting on Authority

The real question we must ask ourselves is: Who's in charge in your world? Who is truly the Lord of your life? In Acts 9, we see a pivotal moment in the life of Saul (later known as Paul), which provides profound insight into this issue. Acts 9:3-5 (NIV) says: "As he neared Damascus on his journey, suddenly a light from heaven flashed around him. 4 He fell to the ground and heard a voice say to him, "Saul, Saul, why do you persecute me?" 5 "Who are you, Lord?" Saul asked.

Saul's response is significant. He asked, "Who are you, Lord?" The term "Lord" is derived from the Greek word "kyrios", meaning "master". It is a term used to denote God or His Son, the Messiah. Despite his initial mission, Paul already knew in his heart that the one he was persecuting was the one truly in charge. This moment of epiphany and salvation was realized when he accepted who was in charge.

Understanding Paul's Transformation

Saul's transformation into Paul marks a profound change in understanding who is in charge. He went from persecuting Christians to becoming one of the most influential apostles, spreading the message of Jesus Christ throughout the known world. This transformation highlights several key lessons:

1. **Acknowledging Authority:** Saul's conversion begins with recognizing and acknowledging the authority of Jesus Christ as Lord. It is a submission to the ultimate authority that changes the trajectory of his life.

2. **Surrendering Control:** Paul's journey teaches us about the importance of surrendering control to God. He let go of his own ambitions and plans to embrace God's will, leading to a life of purpose and impact.

3. **Living Under Authority**: Embracing Christ's lordship means living under His authority, allowing Him to guide and direct our paths. Paul's life exemplifies how acknowledging Jesus as Lord leads to a life aligned with God's purposes.

Personal Reflection: Who's Your Lord?

The struggle over who is in charge is not just an external battle but an internal one as well. We all face moments where we must decide who will be the master of our lives. It's a question of whether we will fight for our own team or submit to God's authority. Matthew 16:24 (NIV) states: "Then Jesus said to his disciples, 'Whoever wants to be my disciple must deny themselves and take up their cross and follow me.'" This verse highlights the need for self-denial and submission to God's authority. True discipleship involves recognizing Jesus as Lord and allowing Him to lead every aspect of our lives.

The Battle Within

In my own life, I've fought for the team "Manny Rivera" many times—too many times. It's a constant battle to surrender my ambitions and desires, learning to let go of the need to be the "king of my mountain." The journey of dying to my ambition has been long and difficult, but it has taught me valuable lessons about submission and trust. Proverbs 3:5-6 (NIV) encourages us to: "Trust in the Lord with all your heart and lean not on your own understanding; in all your ways submit to him, and he will make your paths straight." This passage reminds us to place our trust in God's wisdom and to allow Him to guide our steps. Surrendering control means trusting in His plans and purposes, even when they differ from our own.

Embracing Christ's Lordship

If Jesus is our Lord, then He must be Lord of everything. Acknowledging Christ's lordship means submitting every area of our lives to His authority. It requires letting go of our own agendas and embracing His will, trusting that His plans are for our good and His glory.

Steps to Embrace Christ's Lordship

1. **Recognize His Authority**: Acknowledge Jesus as Lord and submit to His authority in every area of life.

2. **Surrender Control:** Let go of personal ambitions and desires, allowing God's will to guide your path.

3. **Trust in His Wisdom:** Lean not on your understanding but trust in God's plans and purposes for your life.

4. **Seek His Guidance**: Regularly seek God's guidance through prayer, study, and reflection on His Word.

5. **Live Under His Authority:** Align your actions and decisions with God's Word, reflecting His lordship in every aspect of life.

Challenge Questions

1.   Who is truly in charge in your life? Are there areas where you struggle to surrender control to God?

2.   How can you acknowledge Christ's authority in your daily decisions and interactions?

3.   Reflect on a time when you surrendered control to God and experienced His guidance and provision. How can that experience inspire you to trust Him more fully?

The question of who's in charge is a fundamental issue that impacts every area of our lives. As we navigate the complexities of life, let us be reminded of Saul's transformation into Paul and the importance of acknowledging Christ's lordship. Embrace the journey of surrender and trust, knowing that when we allow Jesus to be in charge, we align ourselves with His purposes and experience the fullness of life in Him. Let us commit to making Christ the Lord of our lives, trusting in His wisdom and guidance as we navigate the path He has set before us.

Day 7:

The Sound of the Pressure Cooker

When I was a child, we used to eat dinner at 5:00 pm every day. Occasionally, on the weekends, my parents would push the envelope and serve around 6:00 pm. My mother cooked almost everything from scratch, and being Latin American, pressure cookers were a major part of our culinary arsenal. She used them to cook meat, beans, and vegetables. I vividly remember the sound of the pressure cooker: "che, che, – che, che – che, che" as the metal weight on top of the lid would spin with the steam's pressure.

When I experience periods of high stress and pressure in my life, the image of a pressure cooker often comes to mind. The purpose of a pressure cooker isn't just to cook food but to do so thoroughly, tenderly, and quickly. In a similar way, God, the Master Chef, uses the pressures of life to prepare us, molding us into instruments fit for His purpose.

The Spiritual Pressure Cooker

Throughout the Gospels, we see Jesus navigating His own pressure cookers. His greatest moment of pressure was in the Garden of Gethsemane (Luke 22:39-45). These are the times when pivotal decisions are made that alter destinies and bring about significant change. It was in His pressure cooker that Jesus found the strength and joy to endure the cross (Hebrews 12:2). I am profoundly grateful that Christ chose to do the Father's will in His moment of greatest pressure.

Luke 22:42-44 (NIV) recounts the intensity of this moment: "Father, if you are willing, take this cup from me; yet not my will, but yours be done." An angel from heaven appeared to him and strengthened him. And being in anguish, he prayed more earnestly, and his sweat was like drops of blood falling to the ground.

Personal Pressure Cookers

I can recall numerous times in my life when God threw me into pressure cooker situations. I didn't enjoy them at all. Yet, I now see how these intense periods were designed to shape and prepare me. The Master Chef creates a divine menu to nourish His body and the Church and to bring life to a dying world. God will not serve us to a hungry and desperate humanity unless we've been thoroughly prepared and cooked under pressure. We become nourishment in the Master's hand for people who desperately need it. James 1:2-4 (NIV) reminds us of the purpose behind trials: "Consider it pure joy, my brothers and sisters, whenever you face trials of many kinds, because you know that the testing of your faith produces perseverance. Let perseverance finish its work so that you may be mature and complete, not lacking anything."

Embracing the Process

I find myself, once again, in a season where I hear the sound, che, che, – che, che – che, che… It's time for the pressure cooker once more. I know God is preparing to serve me again to a people hungry for Him. In these moments, my prayer becomes one of surrender and trust. "Lord, let me not escape the pressure situations of life. Let me find my comfort in only fulfilling Your will. Give me joy so I can endure whatever I need to face."

The pressure cooker is not a place of comfort but a place of transformation. Just as a pressure cooker turns raw ingredients into a delicious meal, God uses the pressures of life to turn our raw potential into a refined character that reflects His love and grace. The pressures of life are not meant to destroy us but to refine and prepare us for greater purposes.

Learning from Pressure

God's preparation process through pressure cookers is echoed in many biblical stories. We see it in Joseph's journey from the pit to the palace, Moses's time in the wilderness, and David's years of fleeing Saul. Each of these figures faced intense pressure, yet through it, they were prepared for the roles God had designed for them. Romans 5:3-5 (NIV) speaks to this refining process: "Not only so, but we also glory in our sufferings, because we know that suffering produces perseverance; perseverance, character; and character, hope. And hope does not put us to shame, because God's love has been poured out into our hearts through the Holy Spirit, who has been given to us."

Choosing Joy in Pressure

The sound of the pressure cooker can be daunting, yet it also signals a time of growth and preparation. When we choose to embrace the process, trusting that God is working for our good, we can find joy in the journey. This joy doesn't come from the absence of pressure but from the presence of God within it. Philippians 4:12-13 (NIV) encourages us: "I know what it is to be in need, and I know what it is to have plenty. I have learned the secret of being content in any and every situation, whether well-fed or hungry, whether living in plenty or in want. I can do all this through him who gives me strength."

Application

Reflect on the pressure cookers in your life. Are there areas where you have resisted the pressure, trying to escape instead of embracing the growth it offers? Consider how you can surrender these situations to God, allowing Him to transform you through them.

Spend time in prayer, asking God to give you the strength and joy needed to endure the pressures you face. Seek His guidance in recognizing the lessons and growth opportunities within these experiences.

Challenge Questions

1. How can you reframe your perspective on the pressures in your life, seeing them as opportunities for growth rather than obstacles to avoid?

2. In what ways can you cultivate joy and perseverance in the midst of your pressure cooker situations?

3. Reflect on a time when God used a period of pressure to prepare you for a greater purpose. How can that experience encourage you to trust Him in your current circumstances?

By embracing the sound of the pressure cooker, we allow God to work in and through us, preparing us to be vessels of His grace and love to a world in need. Trust the Master Chef, and know that He is preparing something beautiful and fulfilling in your life. Do you hear the sound? Che, che, – che, che – che, che... It's time to embrace the process and trust in God's perfect plan.

Day 8:

Wrestling with God

Have you ever felt like you have multiple personalities? I sure do. In my morning reading, I came across a scripture that comforted me in my lifelong process of becoming the person God wants me to be.

> *Isaiah 43:1 (NIV)*
> *"But now, this is what the LORD says— he who created you, O Jacob, he who formed you, O Israel: 'Fear not, for I have redeemed you; I have summoned you by name; you are mine.'"*

The Life of Jacob

If you haven't read and studied the life of Jacob, you need to start (beginning in Genesis 25). It's a must for your development process. Jacob began his life as a supplanter, which means someone who lays snares—in other words, he was a trickster and a con artist. This is the actual meaning of the name "Jacob." Of course, he was given this name at birth because of the way he exited his mother's womb.

It seems like we are all born "Jacobs." Take a few moments and do an inventory of your life… need I say more?

From Jacob to Israel

Jacob later became "Israel," which means "God Prevails." You see, God and Jacob had a wrestling match, and yes, you guessed it right—God won! Yep, He always does. Genesis 32:24-28 (NIV) describes this transformative encounter:"- So Jacob was left alone, and a man wrestled with him till daybreak. When the man saw that he could not overpower him, he touched the socket of Jacob's hip so that his hip was wrenched as he wrestled with the man. Then the man said, 'Let me go, for it is daybreak.' But Jacob replied, 'I will not let you go unless you bless me.' The man asked him, 'What is your name?' 'Jacob,' he answered. Then the man said, 'Your name will no longer be Jacob, but Israel, because you have struggled with God and with humans and have overcome.'"

This wrestling match with God was a pivotal moment in Jacob's life. It was here that Jacob, the supplanter, encountered God in a profound way and was given a new identity—Israel, the one who wrestles with God and prevails.

The Wrestling Match

We all need moments in our lives when we face off with God. It's in those moments when, though created as Jacobs, we are formed into "Israels". In other words, the fight in us to self-preserve is lost, and God wins in our lives. We are in a continual process of becoming "Israels."

Wrestling with God is not about overpowering Him; it's about surrendering to His will and allowing Him to transform us. It's about letting go of our old nature and our old identity and embracing the new person God is calling us to be. 2 Corinthians 5:17 (NIV) reminds us of this transformation: "Therefore, if anyone is in Christ, the new creation has come: The old has gone, the new is here!"

Embracing the Process

Hey, cheer up! You were born a Jacob, but you are in a constant process of becoming an Israel. So, don't fear…you have been redeemed and are called by a new name. You are not who you used to be and are continually becoming who you're supposed to be!

God sees beyond our flaws and failures. He sees the potential within us, and through His grace, He molds us into the people He created us to be. This transformation is a lifelong journey, marked by moments of wrestling with God and surrendering to His will.

Lessons from the Wrestling

The wrestling match with God teaches us several important lessons:

1. **Persistence in Prayer**: Jacob's determination not to let go until he received a blessing demonstrates the power of persistent prayer. When we wrestle with God in prayer, we acknowledge our dependence on Him and our desire for His blessings.

2. **Identity Change**: God's question to Jacob, "What is your name?" is a call to self-reflection. It's an invitation to confront our true

selves and allow God to redefine us according to His purposes.

3. Embracing Weakness: Jacob's physical weakness after the encounter—a limp—reminds us that God's strength is made perfect in our weakness. Our struggles and vulnerabilities become the channels through which God's power is displayed.

4. Trusting God's Plan: The wrestling match signifies a transition from self-reliance to trusting in God's plan. It's a call to surrender our own agendas and embrace God's divine purposes for our lives.

The Ongoing Journey

Jacob's story is a reminder that our spiritual journey is an ongoing process of transformation. We may stumble and fall, but God's grace lifts us up and sets us on the path to becoming who He has called us to be. Philippians 1:6 (NIV) assures us of God's faithful work in our lives: "Being confident of this, that he who began a good work in you will carry it on to completion until the day of Christ Jesus."

Application

Reflect on your own wrestling matches with God. Are there areas in your life where you need to surrender and allow God to transform you? Consider how you can embrace your identity as a new creation in Christ, leaving behind the old nature and walking in the newness of life.

Spend time in prayer, asking God to reveal the areas in your heart that need transformation. Seek His guidance in letting go of old patterns and embracing the new identity He has given you.

Challenge Questions

1.   In what ways have you experienced wrestling with God in your life, and how has it led to transformation?

2.   How can you embrace your identity as a new creation in Christ, letting go of the old nature and walking in the newness of life?

3.   Reflect on a time when you experienced a significant change in your relationship with God. How did it impact your understanding of who you are in Him?

By wrestling with God and embracing the transformation He offers, we step into the fullness of our identity as His beloved children. Trust in His plan, and allow Him to mold you into the person He created you to be. Remember, you are not who you used to be, and with God's help, you are continually becoming who you are meant to be.

Day 9:

God Works the BIG out of Your Small

I am a man of BIG DREAMS. At 56 years of age, I realize how important focus is to see those dreams become a reality. I believe I am beginning to learn how to birth out dreams. Before a dream becomes a reality, it is a vision in your spirit. You were created with it already. Focused people have an understanding that when one is operating under the covering of the Kingdom of God, the deposits of greatness that reside inside of them will eventually be released. They also understand that breaking the smallness off of their lives has nothing to do with external circumstances but rather internal transformation.

The Internal Work of God

> *Ephesians 3:20 (NIV) "Now to him who is able to do immeasurably more than all we ask or imagine, according to his power that is at work within us…"*

God's work in us is always "an inside job!" We often direct our attention to what God can and will do—"immeasurably more than we can ask or imagine." But the key to understanding this verse lies in its final words: "according to the power that is working within us." God's bigness and greatness coming out of you is determined by His power that is constantly working in you. In other words, if He is processing you through a time of "small beginnings," your season there is determined by your submission to Him as He works in and through you. Your time of "smallness" is simply put there to cultivate the bigness in you. You are not designed to be small! Do not forsake your smallness—it is the avenue to your bigness!

Embracing Small Beginnings

God often starts with the small to prepare us for the big. The journey from small beginnings to great outcomes is one that requires faithfulness, patience, and trust in God's timing. The seeds of greatness are often planted in the soil of humility and obedience.

> *Job 8:7 (NIV) "Though your beginning was small, yet your latter end would increase abundantly."*

This verse serves as a reminder that God sees the end from the beginning. Our small beginnings are not insignificant to Him; rather, they are part of His divine plan to bring about increase and abundance in our lives. God delights in multiplying the little we have for His glory.

The Process of Growth

Understanding God's Timing

God's timing is perfect, and His process is purposeful. In our eagerness to achieve big dreams, we might rush the process or become frustrated with small beginnings. However, God uses these times to teach us dependence on Him and to refine our character.

> *Ecclesiastes 3:1 (NIV) "There is a time for everything, and a season for every activity under the heavens."*

This verse highlights that every phase of our lives, including the small beginnings, has its purpose and place in God's grand design. Trusting in His timing allows us to embrace each season with grace and patience, knowing that He is working all things for our good and His glory.

Cultivating Faithfulness

Faithfulness in small things is essential to experiencing God's greater works in our lives. When we are faithful with the little He has entrusted to us, He will entrust us with more. Luke 16:10 (NIV)
"Whoever can be trusted with very little can also be trusted with much, and whoever is dishonest with very little will also be dishonest with much." God looks for hearts that are committed to Him, regardless of the size of the task. Our faithfulness in small beginnings prepares us for the greater responsibilities and opportunities He has in store.

Learning and Growing

Small beginnings provide valuable lessons and opportunities for growth. They allow us to develop skills, gain experience, and cultivate a deeper relationship with God. In these moments, we learn to rely on His strength and wisdom rather than our own. James 1:4 (NIV) "Let perseverance finish its work so that you may be mature and complete, not lacking anything."

This verse reminds us that the trials and challenges we face during our small beginnings are shaping us into mature, complete individuals who lack nothing. God uses every experience to build our character and prepare us for the greater things He has planned.

Trusting God's Power Within Us

The Power of God at Work

God's power is not limited by our circumstances or abilities. It is His power working within us that enables us to accomplish more than we can imagine.

Philippians 4:13 (NIV). "I can do all this through him who gives me strength."

This verse reassures us that with God's strength, we can overcome any obstacle and achieve the dreams He has placed in our hearts. His power is the driving force behind our ability to grow and succeed.

Surrendering to God's Process

Surrendering to God's process involves yielding our desires and plans to Him. It means trusting that He knows what is best for us and that His plans are far greater than anything we could conceive. Proverbs 3:5-6 (NIV) "Trust in the Lord with all your heart and lean not on your own understanding; in all your ways submit to him, and he will make your paths straight."

By surrendering to God's process, we allow Him to direct our steps and lead us toward the fulfillment of our dreams. We acknowledge that His ways are higher than ours and that His timing is perfect.

Moving from Small to Big

Breaking Free from Limitations

Breaking free from limitations involves recognizing that God's power within us is greater than any obstacle we face. We must let go of fear, doubt, and insecurity, and embrace the truth that God has destined us for greatness. 2 Timothy 1:7 (NIV) "For the Spirit God gave us does not make us timid, but gives us power, love and self-discipline."

With God's Spirit within us, we can break free from limitations and pursue our dreams with confidence and courage.

Embracing God's Abundance

God desires to bless us abundantly and to use us to bless others. When we embrace His abundance, we become conduits of His love and grace to the world around us. John 10:10 (NIV)
"The thief comes only to steal and kill and destroy; I have come that they may have life, and have it to the full."

God's plan for our lives is one of fullness and abundance. By embracing His abundance, we can impact the world for His glory and experience the joy of living out our purpose.

Application

Reflect on your own journey and consider how God is working the big out of your small. Trust in His timing and embrace each season with faith and gratitude, knowing that He is working all things together for your good and His glory. Remember, you are not designed to be small, and with God's power within you, all things are possible.

Challenge Questions

1. How can you cultivate faithfulness and patience during your small beginnings, trusting that God is preparing you for greater things?

2. In what ways can you surrender your plans to God and embrace His process for growth and transformation?

3. Reflect on a time when God used a small beginning in your life to bring about significant growth or change. How can that experience encourage you to trust Him in your current circumstances?

By seeking to understand how God uses small beginnings, we can trust His plan for our lives and embrace the process of growth and transformation. Through faithfulness, patience, and reliance on His power, we can step into the fullness of our destiny, knowing that He who began a good work in us will carry it on to completion.

Day 10

Know the Author, Know His Author-ity

As I continue to study the subject of prayer, I am learning more about the quality of prayer instead of the quantity of prayer. The quality of prayer lies in understanding how prayer works. It involves realizing our relationship and responsibility in Christ—to ask, decree, and declare the will of God on earth as it is in heaven. According to the Word, God has chosen to involve Himself in the affairs of humanity only in response to our prayers. This divine partnership highlights the importance of knowing the One to whom we pray and understanding His authority.

The Relationship Between the Author and Authority

As I began studying the concept of "authority," I discovered some profound insights. One intriguing discovery was the etymology of the word "authority," which is a derivative of the word "Author." The root behind authority is authorship, not just as in writing but as in creation or origination. In other words, one has authority over what one authors. The creator of a thing determines the purpose of that thing and holds the rights to it. John 1:3 (NIV) "Through him all things were made; without him nothing was made that has been made."

This verse underscores the foundational truth that God is the Creator of all things, and as such, He holds ultimate authority over His creation. Understanding this connection between God's role as Creator and His authority is essential for deepening our prayer life and walking in His power.

The Challenge to God's Authority

The enemy, through theories of macroevolution and humanistic thinking, seeks to dispel our belief in God as the Creator of the universe. By undermining the understanding of God as the Author, these ideologies attempt to weaken our faith in His authority. Colossians 1:16-17 (NIV)
"For in him all things were created: things in heaven and on earth, visible and invisible, whether thrones or powers or rulers or authorities; all things have been created through him and for him. He is before all things, and in him all things hold together."

This passage reaffirms that God is the Creator and Sustainer of all things. If He is not recognized as the Creator of life, then the authority over life is up for grabs. By acknowledging God as the Author, we affirm His rightful authority and align ourselves with His divine order.

Knowing Him, Knowing His Authority

When we truly know God, we will know His authority. This knowledge empowers us to pray with confidence and to live in the fullness of our calling. When we understand authority, not only do the powers of darkness flee, but creation itself will yield to us according to His will. God owns it all; He has all rights of ownership. The choice not to submit to Him is rebellion, but by submitting to Him, we can pray with His authority and legislate through intercession. Romans 11:36 (NIV). "For from him and through him and for him are all things. To him be the glory forever! Amen."

Recognizing God's authority transforms our approach to prayer and life. We are not merely speaking words into the air; we are partnering with the Creator, calling forth His will on earth as it is in heaven.

Walking in Authority

Understanding Our Role

As believers, we are called to walk in the authority of Christ. This means exercising the authority He has given us to bring about His kingdom on earth. Jesus demonstrated this authority during His earthly ministry, healing the sick, casting out demons, and proclaiming the kingdom of God. Matthew 28:18-19 (NIV). "Then Jesus came to them and said, 'All authority in heaven and on earth has been given to me. Therefore go and make disciples of all nations, baptizing them in the name of the Father and of the Son and of the Holy Spirit.'"

Jesus commissions us to go in His authority, continuing the work He began. Understanding and embracing this authority is crucial for fulfilling our mission and living out our purpose.

The Power of Submission

True authority comes from submission to God's will. As we submit to Him, we align ourselves with His purposes and receive the authority to act on His behalf. James 4:7 (NIV). "Submit yourselves, then, to God. Resist the devil, and he will flee from you." Submission to God is the key to resisting the enemy and exercising authority. It is through our relationship with Him that we are empowered to overcome obstacles and advance His kingdom.

The Impact of Authority in Prayer

When we pray with God's authority, our prayers become powerful and effective. We are not begging God to act; we declare His will and partner with Him to bring it to pass. Mark 11:24 (NIV) "Therefore I tell you, whatever you ask for in prayer, believe that you have received it, and it will be yours."

Praying with authority means praying with faith, confident that God hears us and that His power is at work through our prayers. It is about declaring His promises and standing firm in His truth.

Living in Authority

Embracing Our Identity

Living in authority begins with embracing our identity in Christ. We are children of God, heirs to His kingdom, and co-laborers with Christ. Galatians 4:7 (NIV) "So you are no longer a slave, but God's child; and since you are his child, God has made you also an heir." Understanding our identity empowers us to live boldly and to walk in the authority God has given us. We are not powerless; we are equipped to bring about change and to impact the world for His glory.

Exercising Authority in Daily Life

Exercising authority is not limited to prayer; it extends to every area of our lives. We are called to be ambassadors of God's kingdom, reflecting His love and truth in our interactions and decisions. 2 Corinthians 5:20 (NIV). "We are therefore Christ's ambassadors, as though God were making his appeal through us." As ambassadors, we carry the authority of the One who sends us. Our words and actions should reflect His character and advance His purposes in the world.

Application

Reflect on your understanding of God's authority and how it influences your prayer life and daily actions. Seek to deepen your relationship with Him, recognizing Him as the Author and acknowledging His authority in every area of your life.

Challenge Questions

1.   How can you grow in your understanding of God as the Author and His authority over your life and circumstances?

2.   In what ways can you exercise the authority of Christ in your prayers and interactions with others?

3.   Reflect on a time when you experienced the power of God's authority in your life. How did it impact your faith and actions, and how can you continue to walk in that authority?

By knowing the Author, we come to know His authority and our role in His divine plan. Embrace your identity in Christ, submit to His will, and walk in the authority He has given you, knowing that you are empowered to bring about His kingdom on earth.

Day 11

The Knowledge of God

In the fast-paced world we live in, people often struggle to make the right decisions because they lack understanding, even though information is abundant. We are inundated with information from every angle, but possessing information is not enough. The real challenge lies in transforming information into understanding.

The Challenge of Understanding Information

We live in what is often referred to as the "information age," where data and facts are readily accessible at our fingertips. The internet, social media, and various forms of digital communication have created an "information superhighway" where information is constantly being shared and consumed. Yet, despite this abundance, many people struggle to make informed decisions.

As a pastor, I look for knowledge in my leaders. Many talented and intelligent people have crossed my path, but talent and intelligence do not automatically translate into understanding. The key quality I seek is the ability to understand. This ability to understand implies that a person is teachable, open to learning, and willing to grow. It is critical in recruiting leaders who will effectively guide and support others in their spiritual journeys.

The ability to understand is much like the work of a photographer who takes a negative and develops it into a clear photograph. Information, when processed and understood, becomes revelation. This revelation illuminates our purpose and direction, allowing us to navigate life with clarity and wisdom.

Hosea 4:6 (NIV) says, "My people are destroyed for lack of knowledge..." This verse emphasizes the importance of understanding, highlighting that people suffer not merely because they lack information but because they lack understanding.

Understanding vs. Information

In Hebrew, the word for knowledge is da'at, which means to have understanding. Knowledge is the noun, and understanding is the verb. This word is a derivative of yada, which is the Hebrew word meaning "to know Him." It signifies an intimate form of knowing that involves deep, personal experience and connection. Knowing God is not merely an intellectual exercise; it is an intimate, relational understanding that transforms our lives.

When we truly know God, we are actively engaged in knowing Him. This knowing implies a depth of intimacy similar to the connection shared between a husband and wife, encompassing physical, emotional, and spiritual dimensions. Knowing is understanding, and understanding leads to true wisdom.

The Importance of Being Teachable

Being teachable is a crucial component of gaining understanding. A teachable person is open to learning and willing to be guided by others. This quality is essential for anyone who seeks to grow in knowledge and wisdom. Proverbs 1:7 (NIV) says, "The fear of the Lord is the beginning of knowledge, but fools despise wisdom and instruction." A teachable spirit acknowledges the need for guidance and instruction, recognizing that true wisdom begins with a reverence for God.

A teachable leader is one who continually seeks to learn and grow, understanding that no one has all the answers. They are open to receiving feedback, learning from experiences, and applying new insights to their lives. This openness allows them to develop a deeper understanding of God and His ways.

Turning Information into Revelation

Transforming information into revelation requires more than just acquiring facts; it involves seeking God's guidance and allowing His Spirit to illuminate our understanding. Revelation is the moment when God's truth becomes real to us, impacting our lives and directing our paths. James 1:5 (NIV) encourages us, "If any of you lacks wisdom, you should ask God, who gives generously to all without finding fault, and it will be given to you." Seeking God's wisdom is essential for gaining understanding. When we ask God for wisdom, we invite Him to open our eyes and hearts to His truth, transforming information into revelation.

The process of turning information into revelation involves several key steps:

1. **Prayerful Reflection:** Spend time in prayer, asking God to reveal His truth to you. Seek His guidance as you study His Word and reflect on the information you receive.

2. **Meditation on Scripture:** Meditate on God's Word, allowing it to penetrate your heart and mind. The Bible is a source of divine revelation that provides insight and understanding for every aspect of life.

3. **Seeking Godly Counsel:** Surround yourself with wise and godly mentors who can offer guidance and insight. Their experience and perspective can help you process information and gain understanding.

4. **Applying Truth to Life:** Apply the truths you learn to your daily life. As you live out God's principles, you will gain deeper understanding and insight into His ways.

Knowing God Intimately

The ultimate goal of gaining knowledge and understanding is to know God intimately. This knowledge is not merely intellectual but deeply relational. It involves engaging with God in a way that transforms our hearts and minds, aligning us with His purposes. Philippians 3:10 (NIV) says, "I want to know Christ—yes, to know the power of his resurrection and participation in his sufferings, becoming like him in his death." Knowing Christ is about experiencing His presence and power in our lives, allowing Him to shape and mold us into His image.

Intimacy with God leads to greater understanding and wisdom. As we draw closer to Him, we gain insight into His character and ways, equipping us to navigate life's challenges with confidence and grace.

Application

Reflect on your current level of understanding and knowledge. Are you actively seeking to know God more intimately, or have you settled for surface-level information? Consider how you can deepen your relationship with God and pursue greater understanding.

Challenge Questions

1. How can you cultivate a teachable spirit that is open to learning and growing in understanding?

2. In what ways can you transform information into revelation, allowing God's truth to impact your life and decisions?

3. Reflect on a time when you gained a deeper understanding of God's truth. How did it affect your faith and actions, and how can you continue to pursue greater intimacy with God?

By pursuing God's knowledge and seeking deeper understanding, we align ourselves with His purposes and become vessels of His wisdom and truth. Embrace the journey of knowing God, trusting that He will reveal His heart and mind to you as you seek Him with all your heart.

Day 12:

Problem Solvers

Problems are a natural part of life. They arise in every area, from our personal lives to our professional endeavors and even more in our spiritual journeys. While problems are inevitable, how we handle them determines whether they become stumbling blocks or stepping stones. The ability to solve problems effectively is crucial for maintaining momentum and achieving success in any pursuit. When problems are left unresolved, they can become focus breakers, leading to stagnation and frustration. However, by adopting the mindset and qualities of a problem solver, we can navigate challenges with confidence and purpose.

The Nature of Problems

Problems are an inherent aspect of life. They challenge us, test our resilience, and often force us to grow in unexpected ways. While it may be tempting to avoid or ignore problems, doing so can lead to greater difficulties down the line. Instead, we must confront problems head-on and view them as opportunities for growth and learning. By shifting our perspective and embracing the role of a problem solver, we can turn obstacles into opportunities for progress. John 16:33 (NIV) reminds us, "In this world you will have trouble. But take heart! I have overcome the world." Jesus' words assure us that while problems are a part of life, we can find peace and victory through Him.

Qualities of Problem Solvers

Effective problem solvers possess certain qualities that enable them to address challenges with clarity and purpose. By cultivating these qualities, we can enhance our ability to navigate life's inevitable problems.

Anticipating Problems

One key quality of a problem solver is the ability to anticipate problems. This doesn't mean expecting the worst or living in fear of potential issues. Instead, it involves planning ahead and preparing for possible challenges. By thinking proactively, problem solvers can develop strategies and solutions before problems arise.

A problem solver has faith and hopes for the best but plans for the worst. They understand that being prepared is not a lack of faith but a demonstration of wisdom and foresight.

Accepting the Truth

Many people respond to problems by refusing to accept them or by ignoring their existence. However, problems cannot be resolved unless they are acknowledged and faced head-on. A problem solver accepts the truth of a situation, no matter how difficult or uncomfortable it may be.

By accepting the reality of a problem, we can take the necessary steps to address it effectively. Denial only prolongs the issue and prevents us from finding a solution. Proverbs 12:15 (NIV) advises, "The way of fools seems right to them, but the wise listen to advice." Acknowledging the truth allows us to seek wisdom and guidance in solving our problems.

Seeing the Big Picture

Problem solvers maintain a focus on the big picture rather than getting bogged down by obstacles. While it is easy to become overwhelmed by the challenges in front of us, problem solvers keep their eyes on the objectives and goals they wish to achieve.

By seeing the big picture, we can identify the small steps needed to reach our goals. When taken consistently, these small steps lead to significant progress. Luke 16:10 (NIV) teaches, "Whoever can be trusted with very little can also be trusted with much." Focusing on the objectives allows us to be faithful to the small things, which ultimately leads to greater accomplishments.

Handling One Problem at a Time

Problems are rarely solved all at once. Effective problem solvers prioritize issues and address them one by one. By breaking problems down into manageable tasks, we can tackle each one with focus and determination.

Prioritizing problems helps us to concentrate our efforts and avoid feeling overwhelmed. By handling one problem at a time, we can build momentum and achieve success incrementally.

Making Decisions During Peak Times

Important decisions should be made during "peak times," or moments of clarity and strength. Making decisions during times of emotional distress or fatigue can lead to poor judgment and regrettable choices. Psalms 30:5 (NIV) reminds us, "Weeping may remain for a night, but rejoicing comes in the morning." Dark times are temporary, and problems are better solved when we approach them with a clear mind and positive outlook.

By making decisions during peak times, we position ourselves to make wise choices that align with our goals and values.

Turning Problems into Opportunities

The ability to solve problems effectively is not about avoiding challenges but about embracing them as opportunities for growth and learning. Each problem we encounter presents a chance to develop new skills, gain valuable insights, and strengthen our resilience. James 1:2-4 (NIV) encourages us, "Consider it pure joy, my brothers and sisters, whenever you face trials of many kinds, because you know that the testing of your faith produces perseverance. Let perseverance finish its work so that you may be mature and complete, not lacking anything."

By viewing problems as opportunities for growth, we can approach them with a positive mindset and a willingness to learn. This perspective empowers us to overcome obstacles and achieve our goals with confidence.

Application

Reflect on the problems you currently face and consider how you can apply the qualities of a problem solver to address them. Identify one problem you can anticipate and prepare for, and take steps to address it proactively.

Challenge Questions

1. How can you anticipate potential problems in your life and prepare for them with wisdom and foresight?

2. What steps can you take to accept the truth of a problem and address it with honesty and determination?

3. In what ways can you shift your focus from obstacles to objectives, maintaining a clear vision of the big picture?

4. How can you prioritize problems and handle them one at a time, building momentum and achieving success incrementally?

5. What strategies can you use to make important decisions during peak times, ensuring that you approach problems with clarity and strength?

By embracing the qualities of a problem solver, we can navigate life's challenges with grace and determination. With God's guidance and wisdom, we can turn problems into opportunities for growth and transformation, ultimately achieving the goals and purposes He has set before us.

Day 13:

A Sense of Purpose

In the Epistle to the Philippians, Paul exhibits a remarkable sense of purpose that is both inspiring and instructive for all believers. Despite facing imprisonment and physical confinement, Paul never wavered from his goal, purpose, and mission. His unwavering commitment to his calling serves as a powerful reminder of the importance of living with purpose.

Paul's sense of purpose transcended his circumstances. Even though he was in prison, he did not allow his physical containment to suppress his voice or ministry. Instead, he continued to make a difference and enlarge the kingdom of God. His example teaches us that a sense of purpose is not dependent on our external circumstances but rather on our internal commitment to fulfilling God's will.

The Purpose-Driven Life of Paul

Paul's life was characterized by a deep sense of purpose. In Philippians 1:21-26, he writes: "For to me, to live is Christ and to die is gain. If I am to go on living in the body, this will mean fruitful labor for me. Yet what shall I choose? I do not know! I am torn between the two: I desire to depart and be with Christ, which is better by far; but it is more necessary for you that I remain in the body. Convinced of this, I know that I will remain, and I will continue with all of you for your progress and joy in the faith, so that through my being with you again your joy in Christ Jesus will overflow on account of me."

Paul's sense of purpose is evident in his willingness to continue his ministry despite the hardships he faced. He recognized that his life had meaning and significance because of his relationship with Christ and his mission to spread the Gospel.

The Impact of Purpose

A sense of purpose is crucial for living a meaningful and effective life. It provides direction, motivation, and a sense of fulfillment. Without purpose, life can become aimless and unproductive. Paul's life demonstrates several key aspects of living with purpose:

1. **Purpose Motivates You:** A clear sense of purpose drives you to take action and pursue your goals. It fuels your passion and determination, enabling you to overcome obstacles and persevere in the face of challenges.

2. **Purpose Keeps Your Priorities Straight:** When you have a sense of purpose, it becomes easier to focus on what truly matters. It helps you prioritize your time, energy, and resources on activities that align with your goals and values.

3. **Purpose Develops Your Potential:** Living with purpose challenges you to grow and develop your skills and abilities. It pushes you to step outside your comfort zone and strive for excellence in all areas of your life.

4. **Purpose Gives You Power to Live in the Present:** A sense of purpose enables you to live fully in the present moment. It empowers you to make the most of each day and embrace the opportunities that come your way.

5. **Purpose Helps You Evaluate Your Progress:** Purpose provides a framework for assessing your growth and progress. It allows you to measure your achievements and make adjustments as needed to stay on track toward your goals.

The Significance of Leaving a Legacy

George Washington Carver once said, "No individual has any right to come into the world and go out of it without leaving behind him distinct and legitimate reasons for having passed through it." This quote underscores the importance of living with purpose and making a meaningful impact on the world.

Living with purpose is about more than just personal fulfillment; it is about leaving a legacy that reflects God's love and grace. It involves using your gifts, talents, and resources to make a positive difference in the lives of others and contribute to the advancement of God's kingdom.

Embracing Your Purpose

Embracing your purpose begins with understanding who you are in Christ and what He has called you to do. It involves seeking God's guidance and direction for your life and being open to His leading. Here are some steps to help you embrace your purpose:

1. **Seek God's Guidance:** Spend time in prayer and meditation, asking God to reveal His purpose for your life. Seek His wisdom and direction in all your endeavors.

2. **Identify Your Gifts and Talents:** Reflect on the unique gifts and talents God has given you. Consider how you can use them to serve others and fulfill your purpose.

3. **Set Meaningful Goals:** Establish goals that align with your purpose and values. Make a plan to achieve them and take intentional steps toward their realization.

4. **Stay Focused:** Stay committed to your purpose, even when faced with challenges and distractions. Keep your eyes on the bigger picture and trust that God is working in and through you.

5. **Evaluate Your Progress:** Regularly assess your progress and make adjustments as needed. Celebrate your achievements and learn from your setbacks.

Living with a sense of purpose is essential for a fulfilling and impactful life. Paul's example in Philippians demonstrates the power of purpose to motivate, guide, and sustain us, even in the face of adversity. By embracing our God-given purpose, we can make a meaningful difference in the world and leave a lasting legacy that honors God.

Challenge Questions

1.   How can you develop a clearer sense of purpose in your life, and what steps can you take to align your actions with your purpose?

2.   In what ways can you use your gifts and talents to make a positive impact on the world and contribute to God's kingdom?

3.   Reflect on a time when you felt a strong sense of purpose. How did it influence your decisions and actions, and how can you cultivate that same sense of purpose in your current circumstances?

Day 14:

The Habit of Finishing

"It is not how you begin but how you end." This saying underscores the importance of finishing strong in all aspects of life. The ability to finish is key to transitioning properly in life. God will never trust a person with a higher level of living if that person has not been faithful in completing their objectives at the prior level.

Understanding the value of finishing is paramount. A person who diminishes the ethics of finishing will never transition properly to their completed purpose. Purpose is always consummated at death, as one's destiny is a destination. We reach that destination through a journey. Life is that journey, and completed purpose is the end of that journey.

The Value of Finishing

To achieve our destiny, we must develop the habit of finishing. This is not easy, but it is essential. Finishing involves dedication, perseverance, and a commitment to seeing things through to the end. Ecclesiastes 7:8 (NIV) "The end of a matter is better than its beginning, and patience is better than pride." This verse reminds us that the conclusion of a task holds greater value than how it starts, and patience in the process is a virtue we must cultivate.

Developing the Habit of Finishing

Our life in Christ is a series of acts of obedience to directives given to us by God. This could be your calling, your mission—an instruction given by God that will require less of you and more of Him. It will require faithfulness and the giving of your life. We all are given this. It may be in full-time ministry, part-time ministry, volunteer ministry, marketplace ministry, etc. Nevertheless, it is a directive given to a person that becomes part of their identity. The completion of this directive will only cause an evolution of purpose. Obtaining full confidence in knowing one's directive is pivotal, and knowing how to complete that directive is imperative. Philippians 1:6 (NIV) "Being confident of this, that he who began a good work in you will carry it on to completion until the day of

Christ Jesus." This scripture reassures us that God, who started a good work in us, will continue to work in our lives until we reach completion.

Progressing Through Levels

Our purpose is a series of levels. Reaching new levels is only acquired by finishing what was required in the prior level. Graduating from junior high school and entering senior high school can never be achieved unless there is proof of finishing the requirements in junior high school. This principle is duplicated in every aspect of our natural lives. Why, then, does it seem so difficult to practice this in our spiritual lives? New levels will never be achieved until there is a completion at the current level. 2 Timothy 4:7 (NIV) "I have fought the good fight, I have finished the race, I have kept the faith." Paul's words to Timothy illustrate the importance of finishing well. Despite challenges, Paul remained steadfast, finishing the race God set before him.

The Practice of Finishing

Finishing is a habit. Habits determine our future. The practice of finishing is a learned habit that requires intentional effort and discipline.

Steps to Cultivating the Habit of Finishing:

1. **Set Clear Goals:** Define what needs to be accomplished. Without clear goals, it's easy to become distracted or lose motivation.

Proverbs 21:5 (NIV) "The plans of the diligent lead to profit as surely as haste leads to poverty."

2. **Stay Focused:** Keep your eyes on the end goal, even when faced with obstacles or distractions.

Hebrews 12:1-2 (NIV) "Therefore, since we are surrounded by such a great cloud of witnesses, let us throw off everything that hinders and the sin that so easily entangles. And let us run with perseverance the race marked out for us, fixing our eyes on Jesus, the pioneer and perfecter of faith."

3. **Persevere Through Challenges:** Expect challenges and prepare to overcome them. Finishing requires perseverance and determination.

James 1:4 (NIV) "Let perseverance finish its work so that you may be mature and complete, not lacking anything."

4. **Celebrate Small Wins:** Recognize and celebrate progress along the way. Small victories build momentum and encourage continued effort.

Philippians 4:8 (NIV) "Finally, brothers and sisters, whatever is true, whatever is noble, whatever is right, whatever is pure, whatever is lovely, whatever is admirable—if anything is excellent or praiseworthy—think about such things."

5. **Rely on God's Strength**: Seek God's guidance and strength in completing your tasks. He equips us with the ability to finish what we start.

Isaiah 40:29 (NIV) "He gives strength to the weary and increases the power of the weak."

6. **Reflect and Adjust:** Regularly evaluate your progress and make necessary adjustments to stay on course.

Proverbs 16:3 (NIV) "Commit to the Lord whatever you do, and he will establish your plans."

Application

Reflect on areas of your life where you may have left tasks unfinished. Consider how you can develop the habit of finishing in these areas and commit to seeing them through to completion.

Challenge Questions

1. How can you develop the habit of finishing in your spiritual journey and daily life?

2. What steps can you take to ensure that you remain focused and committed to completing your God-given directives?

3. Reflect on a time when you successfully finished a challenging task. How did that experience strengthen your faith and resolve?

By cultivating the habit of finishing, we position ourselves for growth and advancement in our spiritual journey. Let us embrace the discipline of completing what we start, trusting that God will guide us to fulfill our purpose and reach our destiny.

Day 15:

Relinquishment: A Path to True Power and Purpose

Prayer is acquiescence. Prayer is surrender. Prayer is submission. Prayer is relinquishment. As I draw closer to Christ through prayer, the words of John the Baptist resonate more profoundly within me: "He must increase, but I must decrease." (John 3:30)

One of the many paradoxes of the Kingdom of God is relinquishment. Relinquishment involves releasing, yielding, resigning, surrendering, waiving, and giving up something completely. It is through true relinquishment that we engage in power, authority, and our rights as children of God.

The Power of Letting Go

Relinquishment involves letting go of control and allowing God to guide us. When we learn to release the "steering wheel" of our lives and give the Lord full control, we enter into relinquishment. It is then that we can fully embrace our benefits, rights, and privileges as children of God.

Embracing Relinquishment

Our intentions may be good, but our means and methods are often self-centered rather than God-centered. I've been a Christian for 39 years, yet I still strive to fully grasp the concept of total relinquishment. Understanding God's way of doing things gives us access to His means and methods. This can only be achieved through the relinquishment of our entire being. Romans 12:1 (NIV) "Therefore, I urge you, brothers and sisters, in view of God's mercy, to offer your bodies as a living sacrifice, holy and pleasing to God—this is your true and proper worship."

This verse highlights that our act of worship is a living sacrifice, an ongoing process of surrendering our lives to God.

Learning from Moses

Moses is a profound example of the power of relinquishment. He had noble intentions of freeing the Israelites from slavery in Egypt. However, his initial attempts were driven by his own strength and understanding, which led to failure. Only after he relinquished his entire being to God could he fulfill his purpose under God's guidance and authority.

> *Exodus 4:10-12 (NIV) "Moses said to the Lord, 'Pardon your servant, Lord. I have never been eloquent, neither in the past nor since you have spoken to your servant. I am slow of speech and tongue.' The Lord said to him, 'Who gave human beings their mouths? Who makes them deaf or mute? Who gives them sight or makes them blind? Is it not I, the Lord? Now go; I will help you speak and will teach you what to say.'"*

Through Moses's experience, we learn that true power and purpose come when we relinquish our methods and embrace God's ways.

Relinquishment Through Prayer

Relinquishment comes through prayer. The more we pray, the more we realize the need to surrender ourselves to God. Through prayer, we allow God to transform our hearts and minds, aligning our desires and actions with His will.

Steps to Embrace Relinquishment in Prayer:

1. **Seek God's Presence**: Spend time in prayer and reflection, inviting God to reveal areas where you need to relinquish control.

Psalm 46:10 (NIV) "He says, 'Be still, and know that I am God; I will be exalted among the nations, I will be exalted in the earth.'"

2. **Surrender Your Plans:** Offer your desires and plans to God, trusting Him to lead you in the right direction.

Proverbs 3:5-6 (NIV) "Trust in the Lord with all your heart and lean not on your own understanding; in all your ways submit to him, and he will make your paths straight."

3. **Listen for God's Guidance:** Be attentive to God's voice and direction, allowing Him to guide your steps.

Isaiah 30:21 (NIV) "Whether you turn to the right or to the left, your ears will hear a voice behind you, saying, 'This is the way; walk in it.'"

4. **Embrace Humility:** Recognize that relinquishment requires humility and a willingness to acknowledge our limitations.

Philippians 2:3 (NIV) "Do nothing out of selfish ambition or vain conceit. Rather, in humility value others above yourselves."

5. **Trust in God's Sovereignty:** Rest in the knowledge that God is in control and His plans for you are good.

Jeremiah 29:11 (NIV) "For I know the plans I have for you," declares the Lord, "plans to prosper you and not to harm you, plans to give you hope and a future."

Experiencing God's Power and Purpose

As we spend time in our secret place, allow the Lord to teach us to relinquish control. Through prayer and surrender, we experience His power and purpose in our lives by His means and methods. The more we relinquish our will to Him, the more we open ourselves to the transformative work of His Spirit. 2 Corinthians 12:9 (NIV) "But he said to me, 'My grace is sufficient for you, for my power is made perfect in weakness.' Therefore I will boast all the more gladly about my weaknesses so that Christ's power may rest on me." This scripture reminds us that in our weakness and surrender, God's power is made perfect. By relinquishing our control, we allow His strength to manifest in our lives.

Application

Reflect on areas of your life where you need to relinquish control and surrender to God. Spend time in prayer, asking God to reveal these areas and provide the strength and understanding to let go.

Challenge Questions

1.   In what areas of your life do you struggle to relinquish control? How can you surrender these areas to God in prayer?

2.   How can you cultivate a deeper trust in God's sovereignty and guidance through relinquishment?

3.   Reflect on a time when you experienced God's power and purpose through relinquishment. How can that experience inspire you to continue surrendering to Him?

By embracing relinquishment, we align ourselves with God's will and open the door to experiencing His power and purpose in our lives. Let us seek to decrease so that He may increase, trusting that His ways are higher and His plans are perfect.

Day 16:

Praying His Will

In the Epistle to the Colossians, the Apostle Paul emphasizes the critical importance of prayer in discerning and fulfilling the will of God. He highlights the vital connection between knowing God's will and seeking it through prayer. While this may seem simple, I cannot count how many times I have attempted to do God's will without first understanding it through prayer. The will of God requires both right placement and right timing. It cannot be assumed or forced. It is only by seeking it through prayer that we gain a true understanding of it.

The Importance of Prayer in Knowing God's Will

Seeking God's Will Through Prayer

Many times, I've had good intentions, ideas, and strategies, but I executed them in the wrong seasons or places. There have been numerous occasions where I lacked the necessary knowledge, strength, power, endurance, patience, and fruitfulness. These essential qualities come from understanding His will through prayer.

Paul's letters to the Colossians remind us of the importance of continuous prayer to align ourselves with God's will. He writes about praying for the believers to be filled with the knowledge of God's will through spiritual wisdom and understanding.

> *Colossians 1:9-12 (NIV) "For this reason, since the day we heard about you, we have not stopped praying for you and asking God to fill you with the knowledge of his will through all spiritual wisdom and understanding. And we pray this in order that you may live a life worthy of the Lord and may please him in every way: bearing fruit in every good work, growing in the knowledge of God, being strengthened with all power according to his glorious might so that you may have great endurance and patience, and joyfully giving thanks to the Father, who has qualified you to share in the inheritance of the saints in the kingdom of light."*

The Role of Prayer in Gaining Wisdom and Understanding

Prayer is not just a ritual; it is a means to gain insight into God's plans and purposes for our lives. Through prayer, we ask for spiritual wisdom and understanding to live lives that are pleasing to God and bear fruit in every good work.

Paul's prayer for the Colossians includes several key aspects:

1. **Being Filled with Knowledge:** Understanding God's will requires more than human wisdom. It requires divine revelation that comes through prayer. As we seek God's will, we ask Him to fill us with the knowledge of His desires and purposes for us.

2. **Spiritual Wisdom and Understanding:** True wisdom and understanding are spiritual in nature. They come from a deep relationship with God and a commitment to seeking His guidance through prayer.

3. **Living Worthy Lives:** When we know God's will, we can live in a manner that honors Him. Our lives reflect our commitment to His purposes and our desire to please Him.

The Power of Persevering Prayer

Epaphras, a fellow servant of Christ, is commended by Paul for his commitment to prayer. Epaphras wrestled in prayer for the believers, desiring that they stand firm in all the will of God, mature and fully assured. Colossians 4:12 (NIV) "Epaphras, who is one of you and a servant of Christ Jesus, sends greetings. He is always wrestling in prayer for you, that you may stand firm in all the will of God, mature and fully assured."

Epaphras's example teaches us the value of persevering prayer. It shows that knowing and doing God's will often requires persistence and dedication. Wrestling in prayer involves seeking God's will earnestly and not giving up until we have clarity and assurance.

Praying for God's Will in Our Lives

As we pray for God's will, we acknowledge our dependence on His wisdom and guidance. Our prayer is that we may be filled with the knowledge of His will through spiritual wisdom and understanding. Our desire is to fulfill His will in every aspect of our lives, recognizing that His will is our ultimate purpose.

Praying with Purpose

Seeking Wisdom and Understanding: We ask God to grant us insight into His plans and purposes for our lives. This involves a willingness to listen and be guided by His Spirit.

Aligning Our Desires: We pray that our desires align with God's will, allowing His purposes to take precedence in our lives. This requires a heart surrendered to His leading.

Strength for Endurance: We ask for the strength to endure challenges and obstacles that may arise as we seek to fulfill His will. This endurance is fueled by His glorious might and power.

Gratitude and Joy: We offer thanks for the privilege of knowing God's will and participating in His kingdom work. Our gratitude fuels our joy and motivates us to continue pursuing His purposes.

A Prayer for God's Will

Let us pray together:
"Lord, grant me the wisdom and understanding of Your will in my life. May Your will be done in my life as it is in heaven. Fill me with the knowledge of Your desires and purposes, and strengthen me with Your power. Help me to live a life worthy of You, bearing fruit in every good work and growing in the knowledge of You. Give me endurance and patience, and may I joyfully give thanks to You for the inheritance You have prepared for me. Amen."

Challenge Questions

1.   How can you incorporate prayer into your daily routine to seek God's will more consistently?

2.   What steps can you take to ensure that your decisions align with God's purposes for your life?

3.   Reflect on a time when prayer helped you discern God's will. How can you build on that experience to grow in your understanding of His will?

By prioritizing prayer and seeking God's will with wisdom and understanding, we align our lives with His purposes and experience the fullness of His plans for us. Let us commit to praying for His guidance, trusting that He will lead us in the path He has prepared.

DAY 17:

My House Will be Called a House of Prayer

In the Gospel of Mark, Jesus's actions in the temple reveal His zeal for authentic worship and prayer. This passage serves as a powerful reminder of the priority God places on genuine connection with Him, rather than the pursuit of convenience or profit. Understanding Jesus' motivations and the implications for our own lives is essential for cultivating a life centered on prayer.

Jesus' Righteous Anger in the Temple

Mark 11:15-17 (NIV) "On reaching Jerusalem, Jesus entered the temple area and began driving out those who were buying and selling there. He overturned the tables of the moneychangers and the benches of those selling doves, and would not allow anyone to carry merchandise through the temple courts. And as he taught them, he said, 'Is it not written: "My house will be called a house of prayer for all nations"? But you have made it "a den of robbers."'"

During the Passover, many Jews traveled to Jerusalem to offer sacrifices. Because it was often impractical to bring livestock from afar, they purchased animals at the temple. While this system might have seemed convenient, it became exploitative, with merchants charging exorbitant prices. This practice corrupted the temple's purpose, turning it into a marketplace rather than a place of worship.

The Pursuit of Convenience vs. Authentic Worship

1. **Convenience Over Connection:** The practice of selling animals at inflated prices shifted the focus from genuine worship to convenience and profit. The temple, meant to be a place of prayer and communion with God, had become a center for commerce. Jesus' actions underscored the truth that worship and the pursuit of God should never be about convenience.

2. **Seeker-Friendly vs. Spiritual Depth:** Today, churches often

strive to be seeker-friendly, creating environments that are welcoming and accessible. While these efforts are important, they must not come at the expense of deep, authentic worship. We must prioritize cultivating an atmosphere where God's presence is sought above all else. John 4:24 (NIV)

"God is spirit, and his worshipers must worship in the Spirit and in truth."

Why Jesus Was Upset

Jesus' righteous anger was directed at two primary issues:

1. **The Temple's True Purpose:** The temple was intended as a place for prayer and worship, a sacred space where people could encounter God. The commercialization of the temple compromised its purpose and detracted from the holiness of the worship experience.

2. **Exploitation and Profit:** The merchants and moneychangers were exploiting the worshipers, profiting from their devotion. This exploitation was antithetical to the spirit of sacrifice and worship that the temple was meant to embody.

Application to Our Lives

As believers, we are now the temple of God. Paul reminds us of this truth in 1 Corinthians 6:19 (NIV) "Do you not know that your body is a temple of the Holy Spirit, who is in you, whom you have received from God?"

If we are the temple, then the principle still applies: we must be houses of prayer, both corporately and personally.

1. **Examine Your Motivations:** Like the moneychangers, we may unintentionally prioritize personal gain over spiritual growth. We must examine our hearts and ensure that our motivations align with God's purposes.

2. **Prioritize Prayer:** Prayer is the foundation of our relationship with God. It is through prayer that we align ourselves with His will and invite His presence into our lives. We must cultivate a lifestyle of prayer, making it a central part of our daily routine. Philippians 4:6-7 (NIV) "Do not be anxious about anything, but in every situation, by

prayer and petition, with thanksgiving, present your requests to God. And the peace of God, which transcends all understanding, will guard your hearts and your minds in Christ Jesus."

The Call to Be a House of Prayer

Avoiding the Pitfalls of Convenience

- **Spiritual Complacency:** Convenience can lead to complacency, where our spiritual practices become routine rather than transformative. We must guard against allowing convenience to dictate our approach to God.

- **Pursuing God's Presence:** Our primary goal should be to seek God's presence with passion and persistence. We must resist the temptation to prioritize ease and comfort over authentic engagement with Him.

Embracing Authentic Worship

1. **Cultivating a Prayerful Life:** As individuals and as a church, we are called to be houses of prayer. This means dedicating time and effort to cultivate a lifestyle of prayer, both individually and collectively.

2. **Reclaiming Sacred Spaces**: Our bodies and our gatherings are sacred spaces where God desires to dwell. We must reclaim these spaces for His glory, ensuring that our worship is pure and focused on Him.

3. **Aligning with God's Purposes:** We must continually seek to align our lives with God's purposes, allowing Him to guide us in every decision and action. By prioritizing prayer and worship, we invite His guidance and empowerment.

Reflecting on Our Ambitions

God has been challenging my own ambitions and motivations. Like the moneychangers, I have sometimes allowed my desire for success and recognition to overshadow my commitment to God's purposes. I have substituted precious prayer time for pursuits that satisfy my flesh. Matthew 6:33 (NIV) "But seek first his kingdom and his righteousness, and all these things will be given to you as well."

Becoming a House of Prayer

Personal and Corporate Prayer

• **Commitment to Prayer:** We must commit to personal and corporate prayer, making it a priority in our lives. By dedicating time to seek God's face, we create an environment where His presence is welcomed and His purposes are fulfilled.

• **Community of Prayer:** As a church, we are called to be a community of prayer, interceding for one another and for the world. Our gatherings should be characterized by a spirit of prayer and worship, drawing us closer to God and to each other.

Challenge Questions

1. How can you prioritize prayer in your daily life, ensuring that it remains a central focus?

2. In what ways can your church community cultivate a culture of prayer and authentic worship?

3. Reflect on a time when you allowed convenience to overshadow your pursuit of God. How can you realign your priorities to seek Him first?

By committing to prayer and authentic worship, we align ourselves with God's purposes and create an environment where His presence can dwell. Let us embrace the call to be houses of prayer, both individually and collectively, and experience the fullness of His glory in our lives.

Day 18:

Winning

2 Corinthians 2:14 (NIV) "But thanks be to God, who always leads us in triumphal procession in Christ and through us spreads everywhere the fragrance of the knowledge of him."

Understanding that God has designed us to win is fundamental to our faith. As believers, we are fashioned to overcome challenges and experience victory in fulfilling our purpose. This innate ability to triumph is not just about knowing we can win, but also about applying the principles that lead to victory in our daily lives. Here's how we can align ourselves with God's design to be winners.

Understanding Our Design to Win

God, our Creator, has designed us with the ability to win and to be "more than conquerors" through Him. This divine design means that victory is woven into the fabric of our being. Yet, it is not enough to simply acknowledge this truth. We must also have the discipline and determination to apply winning principles in our lives. Romans 8:37 (NIV) "No, in all these things we are more than conquerors through him who loved us."

Even in our failures, we can find victory. Our failures teach us wisdom and understanding, and through them, we learn to trust and rely on God more deeply. Every setback is an opportunity to grow stronger and wiser.

Traits of a Winner in Christ

To truly embody the design to win, we must cultivate certain traits that define winners. Here are two key qualities:

1. Strength in Focus

The ability to focus is crucial for winning. Just as successful athletes must concentrate and block out distractions, believers must maintain focus on their spiritual journey and purpose.

Philippians 3:13-14 (NIV) "Brothers and sisters, I do not consider myself yet to have taken hold of it. But one thing I do: Forgetting what is behind and straining toward what is ahead, I press on toward the goal to win the prize for which God has called me heavenward in Christ Jesus."

- **Overcoming Distractions:** Broken focus often leads to feeling overwhelmed. Distractions can come in various forms, such as criticism, success, setbacks, or applause. A winner remains focused on their ultimate goal and destination.

- **Maintaining Concentration:** Strength lies in the ability to concentrate on the task at hand, regardless of external circumstances. This focus allows us to navigate challenges with clarity and determination.

2. **Ability to Bounce Back**

Resilience, or the ability to bounce back from setbacks, is a defining trait of winners. It enables us to turn failures into launching pads for future success.

2 Corinthians 4:9 (NIV)
"We are hard pressed on every side, but not crushed; perplexed, but not in despair; persecuted, but not abandoned; struck down, but not destroyed."

- **Embracing Failure as Growth:** Winners view failures as opportunities to grow stronger. They use challenges as workouts to build spiritual and emotional muscles.

- **The Resilience of Paul:** The Apostle Paul is an exemplar of resilience. His ability to bounce back from hardships allowed him to write two-thirds of the New Testament and to endure numerous trials for the sake of the Gospel.

Applying Winning Principles in Daily Life

Knowing that we are designed to win, we must actively apply principles that align with this truth. Here's how we can cultivate a winning mindset:

Embracing God's Plan for Victory

- **Trust in God's Leadership:** Acknowledge that God leads us in a triumphal procession in Christ. Trust His guidance in every aspect of life, knowing that He has orchestrated a path to victory for us.

Proverbs 3:5-6 (NIV) "Trust in the Lord with all your heart and lean not on your own understanding; in all your ways submit to him, and he will make your paths straight."

- **Seek God's Wisdom:** Pursue wisdom through prayer and Scripture. Let God's Word illuminate your path and inform your decisions.

James 1:5 (NIV) "If any of you lacks wisdom, you should ask God, who gives generously to all without finding fault, and it will be given to you."

Cultivating a Winning Attitude

- **Stay Focused on Your Goals:** Set clear spiritual and personal goals, and work diligently toward them. Avoid distractions and keep your eyes on the prize that God has set before you.

- **Build Resilience Through Faith:** Develop resilience by leaning on God's strength during trials. Use challenges as opportunities to deepen your faith and reliance on Him.

Challenge Questions

1. How can you strengthen your focus on the goals and purposes God has set for you?

2. In what ways can you build resilience and learn from setbacks to become a stronger winner in Christ?

3. Reflect on a time when you overcame a challenge through faith and perseverance. How did that experience shape your understanding of winning?

Embrace Your Identity as a Winner

Be encouraged today, knowing that you are a winner in Christ. Embrace the qualities of focus and resilience, and trust in God's plan for your life. Remember that even in failures, God is working to teach you and to draw you closer to Him. Let your life be a testament to the victory that is possible through faith in Jesus. Philippians 4:13 (NIV) "I can do all this through him who gives me strength."

By focusing on God's promises and cultivating a resilient spirit, you can walk confidently in the triumphal procession that God has prepared for you. Embrace your identity as a winner and allow God's victory to shine through you, spreading the fragrance of His knowledge everywhere you go.

Day 19:

It's All About Consistency

One of the key principles behind the success of people and organizations is the ability to persevere—to remain productive despite challenging circumstances. Consistent achievement is crucial for realizing desired outcomes. The capacity to apply oneself diligently to tasks is what ultimately leads to the fulfillment of goals. Consistency is about maintaining effort and dedication, even when inspiration is lacking.

The Importance of Consistency

Discipline and Persistence

Consistency requires discipline. Relying solely on inspiration limits our achievements to times when conditions are ideal. Instead, we must be driven by the necessity to fulfill our responsibilities and goals, regardless of our emotional state or external circumstances. Galatians 6:9 (NIV) "Let us not become weary in doing good, for at the proper time we will reap a harvest if we do not give up."

Toughness develops within those who resolve to move forward regardless of feelings or environment. We need to transition from being led by motivation to being moved by the needs around us. In the context of ministry, this means focusing on the spiritual needs of Dade and Broward counties and working consistently to bring people to Christ.

Consistency vs. Mediocrity

Consistency is a mysterious pattern of behavior that distinguishes excellence from mediocrity. Some refer to this principle as "paying your dues," which accurately captures the essence of consistency. No matter how gifted or talented someone is, they will not reach their full potential or fulfill their purpose without consistent effort. Proverbs 12:24 (NIV) "Diligent hands will rule, but laziness ends in forced labor."

Consistency means dedicating time with a clear focus and purpose. Achievers have something tangible to show for their efforts, while others only have consequences of their inaction. As E. Stanley Jones said, "Some people go through life getting results; others get consequences." This emphasizes that without focus and consistency, energy is dissipated, leading to outcomes by default rather than by design.

Moving from Maintenance to Obtaining

As a community, we must transition from maintaining the status quo to actively obtaining our goals and fulfilling our purpose. This shift involves no longer being ruled by circumstances but being guided by our God-given purpose. Philippians 3:14 (NIV) "I press on toward the goal to win the prize for which God has called me heavenward in Christ Jesus."

Power is developed through consistency. This form of power is dynamic, unfolding, unseen, yet undeniably real. Consistent prayer, intercession, and soul-winning efforts are crucial. Let's not abandon the basic instructions God has given us. It's about being consistent in our spiritual disciplines and outreach efforts.

Cultivating Consistency in Our Lives

Setting Clear Goals

To cultivate consistency, it's important to set clear, achievable goals. Having a focus allows us to channel our efforts productively and avoid distractions. Setting both short-term and long-term goals helps maintain momentum and provides motivation to persevere. Habakkuk 2:2 (NIV)
"Then the Lord replied: 'Write down the revelation and make it plain on tablets so that a herald may run with it.'"

By writing down our goals and reviewing them regularly, we can keep our focus aligned with God's purpose for our lives.

Building a Routine

Consistency thrives in routine. Establishing daily habits and routines helps us stay committed to our goals, even when enthusiasm wanes. Regular prayer, Bible study, and intentional community engagement should become integral parts of our daily lives.

> *1 Corinthians 9:24-25 (NIV) "Do you not know that in a race all the runners run, but only one gets the prize? Run in such a way as to get the prize. Everyone who competes in the games goes into strict training. They do it to get a crown that will not last, but we do it to get a crown that will last forever." Training ourselves spiritually and*

mentally through routine prepares us for the challenges we will face and strengthens our resolve to remain consistent.

Accountability and Community Support

Having accountability partners or being part of a supportive community can greatly enhance our ability to remain consistent. Sharing our goals and progress with others creates a network of encouragement and accountability that helps us stay on track. Hebrews 10:24-25 (NIV)
"And let us consider how we may spur one another on toward love and good deeds, not giving up meeting together, as some are in the habit of doing, but encouraging one another—and all the more as you see the Day approaching." Community support provides the encouragement needed to persevere, especially during challenging times.

The Rewards of Consistency

Consistency yields numerous benefits, both spiritually and practically. By maintaining focus and dedication, we can experience growth and transformation in various areas of our lives.

Spiritual Growth and Maturity

Consistency in spiritual disciplines leads to deeper intimacy with God and spiritual maturity. Regular prayer, Bible study, and worship cultivate a strong foundation of faith and enable us to discern God's will more clearly. James 1:4 (NIV) "Let perseverance finish its work so that you may be mature and complete, not lacking anything."

Achievement of Goals

Consistency ensures progress toward our goals. By remaining steadfast, we are more likely to achieve the objectives we set for ourselves, leading to a sense of accomplishment and fulfillment. Proverbs 21:5 (NIV) "The plans of the diligent lead to profit as surely as haste leads to poverty."

Building a Legacy

Consistent effort leaves a lasting impact. By faithfully pursuing our God-given purpose, we leave a legacy of faith and perseverance for future generations to follow.

2 Timothy 4:7 (NIV) "I have fought the good fight, I have finished the race, I have kept the faith."

Embrace the Habit of Consistency

Consistency is a powerful principle that can transform our lives and enable us to fulfill our purpose. By setting clear goals, establishing routines, and seeking accountability, we can cultivate the habit of consistency and experience the rewards it brings.

Challenge Questions:

1. How can you incorporate consistency into your daily spiritual practices?

2. What specific goals can you set to focus your efforts and maintain momentum?

3. How can you seek accountability and support from your community to strengthen your commitment to consistency?

Let us commit to being consistent in our pursuit of God's will, trusting that He will empower us to achieve great things for His Kingdom. Embrace the habit of consistency, knowing that it is the key to unlocking the fullness of God's purpose in our lives.

Day 20:

Prayer and Purpose

The Greek word prothesis, translated as "purpose," is fundamental to understanding our relationship with God through prayer and intercession. It encompasses God's intentions and plans for our lives, our communities, and our world. By grasping the purposes of God, we align our prayers and intercessions with His divine will, enabling us to participate actively in His unfolding plan.

Understanding God's Purpose in Prayer

Prayer and intercession involve declaring, decreeing, and dictating the words authored by God. Through these spiritual activities, we align ourselves with His purposes. This alignment is an act of faith, as emphasized in Hebrews 12:2 (NIV) "Let us fix our eyes on Jesus, the AUTHOR and PERFECTOR of our faith."

Jesus is the Author, the one who designed our lives with intention and purpose. He has written the victory plan for us, and He perfected it. Our lives are perfect creations of God, filled with excitement, adventure, accomplishment, and love. 2 Timothy 1:9 (NIV) "...who has saved us and called us to a holy life—not because of anything we have done but because of his own purpose and grace."

Understanding that our lives are authored by God gives us a sense of destiny. We call it destiny; He calls it purpose. Our journey is about living out the divine script written before time began.

The Role of Purpose in Our Lives

The concept of purpose, derived from the Greek term prothesis, implies setting forth a plan in advance. It is akin to an exposition or thesis describing God's intricate design for our existence. Romans 8:28 (NIV) "And we know that in all things God works for the good of those who love him, who have been called according to his purpose."

God's purpose is preordained. He has written His plan for our lives before we were even born. As stated in Psalms 139:16 (NIV), "Your eyes saw my unformed body. All the days ordained for me were written in your book before one of them came to be." This understanding empowers us to embrace our destiny, knowing that it has been carefully crafted by our Creator.

Aligning with God's Purpose Through Prayer

Prayer and intercession are vital to understanding and living out our purpose. They enable us to connect with the Author of our lives and access the authority He has given us to fulfill His plans.

Declaring God's Will

When we declare God's will in our prayers, we align ourselves with His purposes. This alignment allows us to experience His promises and live out the destiny He has designed for us. Job 22:28 (NIV) "What you decide on will be done, and light will shine on your ways." Declaring God's will through prayer illuminates our path and empowers us to walk confidently in His purpose.

Decreeing God's Promises

Decreeing God's promises involves speaking them into existence. By affirming His truths, we strengthen our faith and invite His power to manifest in our lives. Isaiah 55:11 (NIV) "So is my word that goes out from my mouth: It will not return to me empty but will accomplish what I desire and achieve the purpose for which I sent it." Decreeing God's promises reinforces our commitment to His will and activates His authority in our lives.

Dictating God's Authority

Dictating God's authority means acknowledging His sovereignty over our lives. By submitting to His rule, we allow His power to flow through us and influence the world around us. Matthew 6:10 (NIV) "Your kingdom come, your will be done, on earth as it is in heaven." Dictating God's authority in prayer invites His kingdom to manifest in our lives and our communities, aligning earthly reality with His divine intentions.

Embracing Our God-Given Purpose

Embracing God's purpose involves understanding our unique calling and living it out with intentionality. It requires us to seek His guidance continually and remain open to His leading.

Recognizing Our Calling

Recognizing our calling involves discerning the specific ways God wants us to contribute to His kingdom. This discernment is achieved through prayer and reflection. Ephesians 2:10 (NIV)
"For we are God's handiwork, created in Christ Jesus to do good works, which God prepared in advance for us to do." Understanding our calling empowers us to focus our efforts on fulfilling God's plan for our lives.

Pursuing Our Destiny

Pursuing our destiny requires dedication and perseverance. It involves actively seeking opportunities to serve and glorify God in every aspect of our lives. Philippians 3:14 (NIV) "I press on toward the goal to win the prize for which God has called me heavenward in Christ Jesus." By pursuing our destiny with determination, we align ourselves with God's purposes and experience the fulfillment He promises.

Trusting God's Plan

Trusting God's plan involves surrendering our desires and ambitions to Him. It requires faith in His timing and confidence in His wisdom. Jeremiah 29:11 (NIV) "For I know the plans I have for you," declares the Lord, "plans to prosper you and not to harm you, plans to give you hope and a future." Trusting God's plan allows us to navigate life's uncertainties with peace and assurance, knowing that He is in control.

Living Out God's Purpose

Living out God's purpose is a journey of faith, obedience, and trust. It involves aligning our prayers with His will and embracing the destiny He has prepared for us.

Challenge Questions:

1. How can you align your prayers more closely with God's purposes for your life?

2. In what ways can you declare, decree, and dictate God's will in your daily prayer life?

3. How can you actively pursue your God-given purpose and trust His plan for your future?

As we seek to understand and fulfill God's purposes, let us commit to a life of prayer and intercession, trusting that He will lead us into the fullness of His plan. Embrace the privilege of partnering with God in His work, knowing that His purpose is perfect and His authority is absolute.

Day 21:

The War of Wars

A Confrontation Between Apostles

In Galatians 2:11-21, we witness a compelling confrontation between two Apostles, Paul and Peter. This passage reflects not just a disagreement between two leaders but a deeper war that has been ongoing since the birth of Christianity—a war of cultures, values, and beliefs. It represents the broader Culture War that has influenced and shaped societies throughout history.

Historical Context of Culture Wars

Throughout history, culture wars have been fought between nations and within societies, often over the clash of beliefs, values, and ideologies. Some historical wars have been long and grueling, such as:

- **The Aceh War (1873-1903):** Fought between the Acehnese of Indonesia and the Dutch, lasting 30 years.

- **The Guatemalan Civil War (1960-1996):** A conflict lasting 36 years.

- **The Hundred Years War (1337-1453):** Between England and France, lasting 166 years.

Despite these lengthy conflicts, one war has persisted longer than any recorded in history—the Culture War. This war transcends borders and time, waging between Christian "Kingdom" thinking (Judeo-Christian values) and pagan-humanistic thinking (often aligned with more liberal perspectives).

The Ongoing Culture War

The Culture War is the battle between two dominant worldviews: one rooted in the teachings and values of Christianity and the other in secular, humanistic ideologies. These terms have evolved over time, reflecting societal changes and the shifting landscape of political correctness. In our current era, this war is more pronounced than ever, impacting nations, communities, and individual hearts.

In a multicultural church like ours, these cultural skirmishes often surface as people's traditional values are challenged. The Apostle Paul exemplifies the kind of strong, principled leadership required to navigate such tensions. In Galatians 2, Paul confronts Peter for his hypocrisy, insisting that Christian leaders must stand firm in their faith and not waver, regardless of external pressures or popular opinions.

Paul vs. Peter: A Battle of Beliefs

The confrontation between Paul and Peter was not merely personal but representative of a broader cultural war within the early Christian community. Jewish "Christians" sought to impose their cultural practices, like circumcision, on Gentile believers. Paul's resistance to this cultural imposition was crucial in preserving the integrity of the Christian faith.

> *Galatians 2:11-14 (NIV) "When Cephas came to Antioch, I opposed him to his face, because he stood condemned. For before certain men came from James, he used to eat with the Gentiles. But when they arrived, he began to draw back and separate himself from the Gentiles because he was afraid of those who belonged to the circumcision group. The other Jews joined him in his hypocrisy, so that by their hypocrisy even Barnabas was led astray."*

This passage highlights the cultural and doctrinal battles faced by the early church, illustrating the need for courage and integrity in leadership.

Kingdom Culture vs. Worldly Culture

In the Kingdom of God, there is no room for cultural supremacy or discrimination. When we enter His Kingdom, we surrender our personal and cultural biases, embracing a new identity rooted in Christ. This culture is defined by the teachings of Scripture and the example set by Jesus Philippians 3:20 (NIV) "But our citizenship is in heaven. And we eagerly await a Savior from there, the Lord Jesus Christ."

Our primary allegiance is to God's Kingdom, where His values, morals, and principles guide our lives. This Kingdom culture transcends national, ethnic, and societal boundaries.

The Role of the Church in the Culture War

The church is called to be a beacon of light and truth in the midst of cultural confusion. We are tasked with living out the values of God's Kingdom, breaking down barriers of hostility and promoting unity in diversity. Ephesians 2:14 (NIV) "For he himself is our peace, who has made the two groups one and has destroyed the barrier, the dividing wall of hostility."

As a church, we must actively work to dismantle the walls of racism, prejudice, and division, embodying the love and justice of Christ in our communities.

Winning the War in Our Hearts

The Culture War is fought not only externally but also internally within each of us. It is a battle for our hearts and minds, challenging us to align our lives with God's truth and reject the values of the world that contradict His Word.

Embracing Kingdom Values

To win this war, we must fully embrace the values of God's Kingdom, allowing them to shape our thoughts, actions, and interactions with others. This means prioritizing love, justice, humility, and righteousness over cultural conformity. Romans 12:2 (NIV) "Do not conform to the pattern of this world, but be transformed by the renewing of your mind. Then you will be able to test and approve what God's will is—his good, pleasing and perfect will."

Breaking Down Walls of Hostility

The church has a unique role in healing divisions and fostering reconciliation. By promoting understanding and compassion, we can bridge cultural gaps and create a community that reflects the unity and diversity of God's Kingdom. Colossians 3:11 (NIV) "Here there is no Gentile or Jew, circumcised or uncircumcised, barbarian, Scythian, slave or free, but Christ is all, and is in all."

Standing for Righteousness

We are called to stand firm in our faith and uphold the standards of God's Kingdom, even when it means going against societal norms. This requires courage, conviction, and a deep commitment to the truth of God's Word. 1 Corinthians 16:13-14 (NIV) "Be on your guard; stand firm in the faith; be courageous; be strong. Do everything in love."

Living Out the Kingdom of God

The War of Wars, the ongoing Culture War, is a battle for the hearts and minds of people everywhere. As believers, we are called to live out the Kingdom of

God, embodying His values and principles in a world that desperately needs His truth.

Challenge Questions:

1.   How can you actively embrace and promote Kingdom values in your daily life and interactions with others?

2.   In what ways can you contribute to breaking down barriers of hostility and promoting unity in your community?

3.   How can you stand firm in your faith and uphold God's standards, even when faced with cultural pressures?

As we engage in this war, let us commit to living out the Kingdom of God, trusting that He will empower us to overcome the challenges we face and transform our world for His glory.

Day 22:

God is Looking for God

I learned a lesson from King Asa this morning. If you're not familiar with King Asa, his story is found in 2 Chronicles chapters 14 through 16. The lesson wasn't profound but very sobering. In chapter 15, God used a man named Azariah to speak to King Asa, and it says this:

> *2 Chronicles 15:2 "He went out to meet Asa and said to him, 'Listen to me, Asa and all Judah and Benjamin. The LORD is with you when you are with him. If you seek him, he will be found by you, but if you forsake him, he will forsake you.'"*

These were solemn words spoken to the king concerning prayer. Throughout scripture, God demonstrates a strong attraction to those who seek Him. He promises Asa that if he decides in his heart to pursue God, then God will all the more pursue Asa. This promise is also for us today. You see, in reality, God is looking for God!

God is Searching for Himself in Us

God is searching for Himself in us. He is looking for people who will seek Him. Our promise is that if we seek Him and involve Him in the details of our lives, we will find Him. Pursuing Him denotes you deem Him worthy; you consider Him to be of value and importance. God is attracted to people who give Him entrance. He is on the lookout for Himself in us, and when He connects with us, success, victory, prosperity, fulfillment, and accomplishment are His results.

> *Jeremiah 29:13 (NIV) "You will seek me and find me when you seek me with all your heart." This verse emphasizes the importance of wholehearted pursuit. God desires our complete devotion and promises that those who genuinely seek Him will find Him.*

The Beginning of Asa's Reign

King Asa's reign started with great promise. He sought the Lord wholeheartedly and led significant reforms in Judah. Asa removed idols, repaired the altar of the Lord, and led his people in a covenant to seek the Lord with all their heart and soul.

2 Chronicles 14:2-4 (NIV) "Asa did what was good and right in the eyes of the LORD his God. He removed the foreign altars and the high places, smashed the sacred stones, and cut down the Asherah poles. He commanded Judah to seek the LORD, the God of their ancestors, and to obey his laws and commands."

This passage demonstrates Asa's commitment to God at the beginning of his reign. His dedication brought peace and prosperity to Judah.

The Consequences of Forsaking God

Unfortunately, Asa's story did not end well. Despite his early success in reforming Israel, he could not maintain his devotion to God. As his kingdom prospered, Asa gradually relied more on human wisdom and alliances than on seeking God's guidance.

He faced a significant challenge when Baasha, king of Israel, fortified Ramah to prevent anyone from leaving or entering Judah. Instead of seeking the Lord as he had done before, Asa turned to Ben-Hadad, king of Aram, for help, forming an alliance by offering treasures from the temple.

2 Chronicles 16:7-9 (NIV) "At that time Hanani the seer came to Asa king of Judah and said to him, 'Because you relied on the king of Aram and not on the LORD your God, the army of the king of Aram has escaped from your hand. Were not the Cushites and Libyans a mighty army with great numbers of chariots and horsemen? Yet when you relied on the LORD, he delivered them into your hand. For the eyes of the LORD range throughout the earth to strengthen those whose hearts are fully committed to him. You have done a foolish thing, and from now on you will be at war.'"

The Importance of Finishing Well

Asa's story teaches us about the dangers of losing sight of God amid blessings and success. Despite his initial faithfulness, Asa's reliance on human alliances led to his downfall. God gave him another opportunity to reconsider his ways and return to seeking Him, but Asa refused. He became angry with Hanani, imprisoned him, and oppressed some of the people.

2 Chronicles 16:12 (NIV) "In the thirty-ninth year of his reign Asa was afflicted with a disease in his feet. Though his disease was severe, even in his illness he did not seek help from the LORD, but only from the physicians."

Asa's refusal to seek God, even in his illness, serves as a warning to us. It's not enough to start well; we must finish well by maintaining our devotion to God throughout our lives.

God's Promise to Those Who Seek Him

God is looking for Himself in us! He wants us to finish well. We cannot continue in our journey without His presence. When we seek Him, we will find Him. He is searching for us, and we are to search for Him. When we find each other, oh what a partnership that will be!

> *Matthew 7:7-8 (NIV) "Ask and it will be given to you; seek and you will find; knock and the door will be opened to you. For everyone who asks receives; the one who seeks finds; and to the one who knocks, the door will be opened."*

God promises to be found by those who earnestly seek Him. He desires a relationship with us and is eager to reveal Himself to those who pursue Him wholeheartedly.

The Call to Seek God

As we reflect on King Asa's story, let us commit to seeking God with all our hearts. Let us not rely on our strength or wisdom but on His guidance and presence in every aspect of our lives. By seeking God, we align ourselves with His will and experience the fullness of His blessings.

Challenge Questions:

1.   How can you actively seek God in your daily life and involve Him in your decisions and plans?

2.   What areas of your life have you relied on your strength or human wisdom instead of seeking God's guidance?

3.   Reflect on a time when you experienced God's presence and blessings as a result of seeking Him. How can that experience inspire you to continue pursuing Him wholeheartedly?

Let us heed the lessons from Asa's life and strive to finish well by maintaining a steadfast commitment to seeking God. As we do so, we will discover the profound joy and fulfillment that come from a deep and abiding relationship with our Creator. May we be a people whose hearts are fully committed to Him, experiencing the strength and blessings He promises to those who seek Him earnestly.

Day 23:

The Purpose of the Law

Before we can fully comprehend the redemption that Christ offers, we must first understand the purpose of the law. This foundational knowledge is crucial for grasping the significance of what Jesus accomplished for us. When we talk about the "Law," we're referring to the initial Ten Commandments and the broader system of laws given to Israel in the Old Testament. Here are a few examples of the purpose of the law:

1. The Law Shows Our Guilt Before God

The law serves to highlight our guilt before God and prevents us from justifying ourselves. It acts as a mirror, reflecting our shortcomings and imperfections, revealing our need for a savior. Romans 3:19 (Amplified) "Now we know that whatever the Law says, it speaks to those who are under the Law, so that [the murmurs and excuses of] every mouth may be hushed and the entire world may be held accountable to God."

The law reveals our inability to live up to God's standards and silences any excuses we might offer. It shows us that we are accountable to God for our actions.

2. The Law Brings Us to the Knowledge of Sin

The law helps us become conscious of sin. It makes us aware of our moral failures and the ways in which we fall short of God's holiness. Romans 3:20 (NIV) "Therefore no one will be declared righteous in his sight by observing the law; rather, through the law we become conscious of sin." Through the law, we gain an awareness of our sinfulness, which highlights our need for redemption and forgiveness.

3. The Law Defines Sin

The law provides a clear definition of sin. Without it, we would not have a full understanding of what is right and wrong according to God's standards. Romans 7:7 (NIV) "What shall we say, then? Is the law sin? Certainly not! Indeed I would not have known what sin was except through the law. For I would not have known what coveting really was if the law had not said, 'Do not covet.'"

The Apostle Paul explains that the law is not sinful; rather, it reveals what sin is. It helps us recognize our transgressions by setting a standard for righteousness.

4. The Law Leads Us to Christ

The law was designed to guide us to Christ, serving as a tutor or guardian until He came. It shows us our need for salvation and points us toward the grace and mercy offered through Jesus. Galatians 3:24 (Amplified) "So that the Law served [to us Jews] as our trainer [our guardian, our guide to Christ, to lead us] until Christ [came], that we might be justified (declared righteous, put in right standing with God) by and through faith."

The law serves as a guide that leads us to Jesus, the one who can fulfill its requirements and provide the redemption we desperately need.

5. The Law as a Teacher and Guide

The Bible says in Psalm 19:7 "The law of the Lord is perfect, converting the soul."

The law serves as a teacher and guide, leading us to recognize our need for a savior. It reveals our sinfulness and directs us to Jesus, who can redeem us from the law's demands. The true understanding of the law should drive us to our knees in repentance, recognizing our need for God's grace and mercy.

When we share our faith, explaining the purpose of the law can help others understand the need for repentance and the significance of Christ's sacrifice. The law is not just a set of rules but a divine tool that brings us to a greater understanding of our need for redemption through Jesus Christ.

Challenge Questions

1. How does understanding the purpose of the law deepen your appreciation for Christ's redemption?

2. In what ways can you use the knowledge of the law to explain the need for salvation to others?

3. Reflect on a time when the law revealed your need for God's grace. How did that experience lead you to a deeper relationship with Christ?

By understanding the purpose of the law, we can more fully appreciate the grace and redemption offered through Jesus Christ. Let this knowledge deepen our faith and inspire us to share the good news with others, leading them to the hope and salvation found in Him alone.

Day 24:

When Paying the Price Pays Back

"Jesus looked at them and said, 'With man this is impossible, but not with God; all things are possible with God.'" (Mark 10:27, NIV)

This verse from Mark is a powerful declaration about the power of God to work within our temporal impossibilities. Yet, while we often quote this scripture when seeking God's help for resources, favor, or possessions, we tend to overlook its original context. Understanding the context reveals a profound truth about the nature of true discipleship and the sacrifices involved in following Jesus.

Understanding the Context

The verse emerges from Jesus' encounter with the Rich Young Ruler, which is recounted in Mark 10:17-29. The Rich Young Ruler approached Jesus, asking what he must do to inherit eternal life. Despite his adherence to the commandments, he struggled to surrender his wealth, leading to Jesus' observation:

> *Mark 10:25, NIV "It is easier for a camel to go through the eye of a needle than for a rich man to enter the kingdom of God."*

His disciples, perplexed, asked, "Who then can be saved?" This was the moment Jesus spoke the words, "With man this is impossible, but not with God; all things are possible with God."

The context here is about the cost of discipleship and the impossibility of attaining the Kingdom of God through self-righteousness or personal effort alone. Jesus wasn't denouncing wealth but highlighting the difficulty of prioritizing the Kingdom over worldly possessions.

The Cost of Discipleship

Self-Righteousness vs. Humble Submission

The Rich Young Ruler exemplifies the struggle many face when asked to prioritize their spiritual journey over material wealth. He initially believed he could earn eternal life through his adherence to religious laws. Jesus, however, reveals that genuine discipleship requires a deeper sacrifice:

131

- **Surrendering Possessions:** True discipleship calls us to release our grip on material wealth and instead focus on spiritual richness. Jesus invites us to live with open hands, willing to give up everything for the sake of the Gospel.

- **Embracing Humility:** We must recognize our limitations and acknowledge our reliance on God. Our efforts alone cannot secure eternal life; it is through God's grace and power that we find salvation.

Entering God's Realm of Possibilities

In surrendering our own desires and ambitions, we enter into God's realm of possibilities. This shift in focus allows us to see beyond our limitations and embrace the life God intends for us. Jesus promises that those who sacrifice for His sake will not only receive rewards in the life to come but also experience His blessings here and now.

Living in God's Possibilities

The Reward of Faithful Living

Jesus assures us that when we pay the price to follow Him, the rewards are abundant. This promise extends beyond the material realm and touches every aspect of our lives:

- **Spiritual Richness:** We gain deeper intimacy with God, experiencing His peace, joy, and love more profoundly.

- **Purpose and Fulfillment:** We discover our true calling and purpose in serving God and others.

- **Eternal Perspective:** Our focus shifts from temporary gains to eternal significance, aligning our actions with God's will.

The Principle of Reciprocity

In God's Kingdom, paying the price of discipleship leads to a divine exchange. We relinquish temporary pleasures and receive eternal rewards. Jesus promises:

"Truly I tell you, no one who has left home or brothers or sisters or mother or father or children or fields for me and the gospel will fail to receive a hundred times as much in this present age: homes, brothers, sisters, mothers, children and fields—along with persecutions—and in the age to come eternal life." (Mark 10:29-30, NIV)

This principle underscores the truth that God's generosity exceeds our expectations, providing not only for our spiritual needs but also for our earthly ones.

Embracing the Call

Practical Steps to Prioritize God's Kingdom

- **Evaluate Your Priorities:** Reflect on what occupies your thoughts and time. Are you prioritizing material wealth or spiritual growth?

- **Practice Generosity:** Cultivate a habit of giving, both financially and in acts of service, to reflect the heart of Christ.

- **Seek God's Guidance:** Pray for wisdom and discernment to make choices that align with His will.

The Power of God's Promises

When we commit to following Christ wholeheartedly, we experience the transformative power of God's promises. His faithfulness assures us that even in sacrifice, we are never left lacking.

Challenge Questions

1. What are the areas in your life where you need to surrender control and trust God's provision?

2. How can you cultivate a heart of generosity that prioritizes God's Kingdom over material possessions?

3. Reflect on a time when you experienced God's provision after making a sacrifice for His Kingdom. How did it impact your faith journey?

The story of the Rich Young Ruler reminds us of the importance of surrendering our desires to embrace the life God has planned for us. When we pay the price of discipleship, we enter God's realm of possibilities, experiencing His abundant blessings in every aspect of our lives. Let us embrace this truth, trusting that when we prioritize God's Kingdom, He will provide for all our needs and reward us beyond measure.

Day 25:

The Art of Remembering

"Wisdom is supreme; therefore get wisdom. Though it cost all you have, get understanding." (Proverbs 4:7, NIV)

Wisdom is a treasure that surpasses material wealth in value. It is the knowledge and experience needed to make sensible decisions and judgments, derived from accumulated knowledge of life or in a particular sphere of activity gained through experience. But how does one acquire wisdom, and what role does memory play in this process?

Understanding Wisdom

The Nature of Wisdom

Wisdom is more than just knowledge; it is the ability to apply knowledge effectively in real-life situations. It involves discernment and insight, enabling us to make sound decisions.

- **Knowledge vs. Wisdom:** Knowledge is the accumulation of facts and information, while wisdom is the practical application of that knowledge.

- **Experience as a Teacher:** Life experiences are the primary source of wisdom. However, merely living through experiences does not guarantee wisdom. Reflection and learning from these experiences are crucial.

Acquiring Wisdom

Proverbs 4:7 emphasizes the importance of acquiring wisdom, even at great personal cost. This suggests that wisdom requires intentional effort and investment.

- **The Price of Wisdom:** Acquiring wisdom involves a conscious decision to prioritize learning and growth. This might mean sacrificing time, energy, and resources to pursue understanding.

- **Exchange for Wisdom:** The exchange involves letting go of ignorance and embracing the lessons life offers.

The Role of Memory in Wisdom

The Art of Remembering

The process of remembering plays a crucial role in the acquisition of wisdom. It involves the discipline to remember what is important and forget what is not.

- **Selective Memory:** We must train ourselves to remember the lessons that shape us positively and forget the negative experiences that hold us back.

- **Holy Spirit's Role:** The Holy Spirit aids in reminding us of God's teachings and lessons from our experiences.

"But the Helper, the Holy Spirit, whom the Father will send in my name, will teach you all things and bring to your remembrance all that I have said to you." (John 14:26, ESV)

Remembering the Right Things

C.S. Lewis has said, "We often remember what we should forget and forget what we should remember. Correcting this tendency can lead to greater wisdom."

- **Translating Short-Term to Long-Term Memory:** By committing significant lessons and experiences to long-term memory, we ensure they inform our future decisions.

- **The Role of Encouragement:** Encouragement from others can serve as a reminder of past victories and God's faithfulness, reinforcing the wisdom we have gained.

Forgetting the Wrong Things

- **Letting Go of the Negative:** Holding on to past failures or hurts can cloud judgment and impede wisdom. Forgetting these allows for a clearer focus on God's truth.

C.S. Lewis has also said, "We need to be reminded more than instructed." This implies that recalling past lessons is often more valuable than seeking new information.

The Practice of Remembering

Practical Steps

1. **Reflect Regularly:** Take time to reflect on past experiences and identify key lessons.

2. **Journal Your Insights:** Writing down insights and reflections helps solidify them in your memory.

3. **Engage in Prayer and Meditation:** Seek the Holy Spirit's guidance to remind you of important truths and lessons.

4. **Surround Yourself with Encouragement:** Engage with people who uplift and remind you of God's faithfulness.

The Outcome of Remembering

When we effectively remember, we tap into a reservoir of wisdom that guides our decisions and actions. Remembering God's past faithfulness builds faith for the future.

- **Accessing Godly Wisdom:** Remembering aligns our thoughts with God's wisdom, leading to sound decisions.

- **Staying the Course:** Remembrance fuels perseverance, reminding us that if God acted in the past, He will do so again.

Challenge Questions

1. What are some key lessons or experiences from your past that you need to remember to access wisdom?

2. How can you practice the discipline of remembering important truths and forgetting negative experiences?

3. In what ways can you invite the Holy Spirit to guide your memory and enhance your wisdom?

The art of remembering is a vital component of acquiring and applying wisdom. By selectively remembering what is beneficial and forgetting what is detrimental, we align ourselves with God's wisdom and guidance. Let us embrace the discipline of memory, trusting that God will use it to lead us into a deeper understanding and greater fulfillment of His purpose in our lives. Through prayer, reflection, and encouragement, we can cultivate a habit of remembering that enriches our journey with wisdom and understanding.

Day 26:

Your Fave 5

Our circle of influence encompasses the people who significantly affect our lives and whom we, in turn, impact. Everyone has a circle of influence, but within that circle, there are varying levels of influence, with the core group usually consisting of about five people. These five individuals, your "Fave 5," have a profound impact on your life, shaping who you are and who you become.

The Power of Your Fave 5

The concept of your Fave 5 highlights the importance of relationships in our personal development. Business philosopher Jim Rohn famously said, "We become the combined average of the five people we associate with most." This insight underlines how deeply intertwined our lives are with those we spend the most time with.

Key Areas of Influence

- **Finances:** The financial habits and perspectives of your closest circle often reflect in your financial status and decisions.

- **Health:** Your Fave 5 can influence your lifestyle choices, including diet, exercise, and overall well-being.

- **Career:** Career ambitions, ethics, and work habits are often shared and reinforced within your core group.

- **Self-Esteem:** The quality of encouragement and support you receive impacts your confidence and self-worth.

- **Habits:** Whether positive or negative, habits tend to be shared or influenced by those closest to you.

- **Values and Goals:** The shared values and aspirations within your group can shape your priorities and life direction.

Evaluating Your Circle of Influence

Understanding the impact of your Fave 5 can lead to conscious decisions about who you allow to influence your life. It is essential to assess whether these relationships are pulling you up, pulling you down, or keeping you in neutral.

Steps to Evaluate and Adjust Your Circle

1. **Reflect on Your Relationship**s: Identify the five people you spend the most time with and consider how they influence various aspects of your life.

2. **Assess the Direction of Influence:** Determine whether these individuals are encouraging growth and positive change or fostering stagnation and negativity.

3. **Seek Growth-Oriented Relationships:** Surround yourself with people who inspire and challenge you to pursue your purpose in Christ and personal development.

4. **Be a Positive Influence**: Consider how you impact your Fave 5. Are you encouraging them in their growth and journey, or are you holding them back?

5. **Make Necessary Changes:** If certain relationships are detrimental to your growth, it may be time to reevaluate and adjust your circle of influence.

Upgrading Your Circle

The process of upgrading your circle of influence involves being intentional about the relationships you cultivate. This does not mean abandoning existing friendships but rather seeking relationships that align with your values and goals.

Benefits of Upgrading

• **Enhanced Growth:** Being surrounded by growth-minded individuals encourages continuous personal and spiritual development.

• **Increased Motivation:** Positive influences can reignite your passion and drive, pushing you towards achieving your goals.

• **Strengthened Values:** Aligning with people who share your values reinforces your commitment to those principles.

- **Expanded Opportunities:** Networking with influential and successful individuals can open doors to new opportunities and experiences.

Biblical Perspective on Relationships

The Bible offers wisdom on the importance of choosing our companions wisely.

Proverbs 13:20 (NIV): "Walk with the wise and become wise, for a companion of fools suffers harm."

1 Corinthians 15:33 (NIV): "Do not be misled: 'Bad company corrupts good character.'"

These verses emphasize the importance of surrounding ourselves with individuals who reflect the wisdom and character we aspire to develop.

Challenge Questions

1. Who are the five people you spend the most time with, and how do they influence your life?

2. Are there relationships in your life that need to be reevaluated to align more closely with your values and goals?

3. How can you be a positive influence within your circle, encouraging growth and development in those around you?

The people we choose to surround ourselves with have a significant impact on our lives. By being intentional about our Fave 5, we can create a circle of influence that inspires growth, aligns with our values, and propels us towards our God-given purpose. Take the time to evaluate your relationships and ensure they reflect the direction you want your life to take. Remember, your Fave 5 should be a source of encouragement and inspiration, helping you to become the best version of yourself.

Day 27:

Want to be Famous?

"Then His fame went throughout all Syria; and they brought to Him all sick people who were afflicted with various diseases and torments, and those who were demon-possessed, epileptics, and paralytics; and He healed them." (Matthew 4:24 NIV)

As a child, I often dreamed of being famous. I imagined myself in the spotlight, hearing crowds chant my name for achievements in sports, music, or acting. I was so convinced of my potential fame that I would confidently tell my classmates, "You'll see, I'll be world-famous one day!" I believe that a child's aspiration to be famous is not merely an unreachable fantasy but an innate God-given attribute within their designed purpose to influence and affect many lives.

Now, at the age of 56, I'm realizing that dreams do come true—but not always in the way we imagined. Everyone has the potential to be famous, but fame is a relative term. The choice lies in whether we want to be famous before God or famous before people. Personally, I choose God.

Biblical Fame: Significance Over Prominence

Biblical fame is not about prominence but about significance. It is about making an impact where it matters most. When we desire to do great things for Him and not for ourselves, God often places us on platforms where we can radiate His glory. As John the Baptist expressed, "He must increase, but I must decrease" (John 3:30).

Significance in the Kingdom

In the end, I believe many people will be declared famous by God who were not prominent on earth. These will be individuals who were obedient, allowing themselves to be formed and shaped to be significant to the Kingdom of God in the place He placed them.

Chris Tomlin captured this beautifully in his worship song, "The Famous One":

143

You are the Lord / The famous one, Famous one / Great is your name / In all the earth / the heavens declare / You're glorious, glorious / Great is your fame beyond the earth...

The Pursuit of Godly Fame

The pursuit of godly fame requires a shift in perspective. Instead of seeking personal glory, we seek to glorify Him. This involves allowing God to work through us to positively impact others.

Ways to Pursue Godly Fame:

1. **Serve Others**: Jesus' fame spread not because of His pursuit of renown but because of His service to others. By serving others selflessly, we reflect Christ's love and spread His fame.

2. **Share His Message:** Like the early disciples, we are called to spread the gospel. Our lives should be a testament to His transformative power, drawing others to Him.

3. **Reflect His Character:** Living a life that mirrors Christ's character—humility, love, and integrity—brings glory to His name.

4. **Pursue Excellence:** Whatever we do, we do it for the glory of God. By striving for excellence in our work and relationships, we honor Him.

5. **Seek Obedience**: Our obedience to God's calling is what truly makes us significant in His Kingdom.

The Impact of a Life Lived for God

Living for God does not always lead to worldly fame, but it leads to something far greater: eternal significance. As we live out our faith, we become a part of His story, contributing to His eternal purposes.

The Eternal Perspective

Paul reminds us in Colossians 3:2-4 (NIV) "Set your minds on things above, not on earthly things. For you died, and your life is now hidden with Christ in God. When Christ, who is your life, appears, then you also will appear with him in glory."

Our ultimate reward is not in earthly fame but in the eternal glory that comes from being aligned with God's purposes.

Challenge Questions

1.   How can you shift your focus from seeking personal fame to seeking significance in God's Kingdom?

2.   In what ways can you spread the fame of Christ in your everyday life?

3.   Reflect on someone you know who is significant in God's Kingdom but not necessarily famous in the world. What qualities do they exhibit that you can emulate?

The more I desire to be privately significant for Him, the more He gives me the humbling privilege of being prominent in His Kingdom. We all have the responsibility to spread the fame of Christ by the very lives we live. In doing so, we fulfill our God-given purpose and leave a lasting impact on the world around us.

He is the Famous One, and as we reflect His glory, we become a part of His eternal story. Let's live for the fame of Christ, trusting that He will use our lives to bring glory to His name.

Day 28:

King Herod's Blunder: The True Nature of Seeking and Worship

Matthew 2:7-8 (NIV) Then Herod called the Magi secretly and found out from them the exact time the star had appeared. He sent them to Bethlehem and said, "Go and make a careful search for the child. As soon as you find him, report to me, so that I too may go and worship him."

In this passage, King Herod instructs the Magi to find the newborn King and report back to him, under the guise of wanting to worship Him. However, Herod's intentions were far from genuine worship. This encounter reveals deeper truths about the nature of seeking God and the authenticity required for true worship.

The Essence of Seeking and Pursuit

Psalm 27:4 (NIV) "One thing I ask from the LORD, this only do I seek: that I may dwell in the house of the LORD all the days of my life, to gaze on the beauty of the LORD and to seek him in his temple."

Seeking God involves a proactive and passionate endeavor, transforming mere desire into purposeful action. King David exemplifies this in Psalm 27:4, where he expresses his deepest longing to seek the Lord. True seeking requires action and intentional pursuit, transforming our spiritual desires into a journey toward God.

Matthew 7:7-8 (NIV) "Ask and it will be given to you; seek and you will find; knock and the door will be opened to you. For everyone who asks receives; the one who seeks finds; and to the one who knocks, the door will be opened."

This scripture illustrates the promise that seeking leads to finding. When we actively pursue God, He is faithful to reveal Himself to us.

Herod's Misguided Intentions

Herod's request to the Magi was deceptive. His intention was not to worship but to eliminate a perceived threat to his throne. This highlights the importance

147

of personal engagement in worship. Authentic worship cannot be mediated by others; it requires direct and personal pursuit.

> *James 4:8 (NIV) "Come near to God and he will come near to you. Wash your hands, you sinners, and purify your hearts, you double-minded." James reminds us that drawing near to God is a personal act that requires sincerity and purity of heart. Herod's failure to seek God personally reveals the importance of genuine desire in worship.*

The Innate Yearning to Seek

The human soul possesses an intrinsic drive to seek its Creator, reflecting a fundamental principle of creation: separation from the source leads to death. Just as plants perish without soil and fish without water, humans experience spiritual death when disconnected from God.

> *Acts 17:27-28 (NIV) "God did this so that they would seek him and perhaps reach out for him and find him, though he is not far from any one of us. 'For in him we live and move and have our being.'*

This passage emphasizes the closeness of God and the innate human drive to seek Him, underlining the importance of maintaining a connection with our Creator.

Worship: Beyond Lip Service

Herod's request to have the Magi find the Christ child on his behalf underscores the danger of superficial worship. Authentic worship requires personal engagement and commitment.

> *John 4:23-24 (NIV) "Yet a time is coming and has now come when the true worshipers will worship the Father in the Spirit and in truth, for they are the kind of worshipers the Father seeks. God is spirit, and his worshipers must worship in the Spirit and in truth." True worship requires sincerity and personal involvement, as highlighted by Jesus in His conversation with the Samaritan woman. Worship in spirit and truth demands authenticity and an earnest pursuit of God.*

What We Seek, We Worship

Herod's story underscores a profound truth: we become what we seek. Our pursuits reflect our deepest desires and priorities. Whatever we earnestly seek becomes the object of our worship.

Matthew 6:21 (NIV) "For where your treasure is, there your heart will be also." This passage challenges us to evaluate our pursuits and consider whether they align with our commitment to God. Our desires shape our actions and ultimately, our worship.

The Magi's Example of True Worship

The Magi demonstrate genuine pursuit by traveling great distances to seek the Christ child. Their journey is marked by dedication, sacrifice, and a sincere desire to worship.

Matthew 2:10-11 (NIV) "When they saw the star, they were overjoyed. On coming to the house, they saw the child with his mother Mary, and they bowed down and worshiped him. Then they opened their treasures and presented him with gifts of gold, frankincense, and myrrh." The Magi's example challenges us to embrace the journey of seeking God with the same fervor and commitment, recognizing that true worship requires active engagement and sacrifice.

Embracing the Call to Seek

The call to seek God is a lifelong invitation, a journey of discovery, growth, and transformation. As we embark on this journey, we are reminded that the pursuit itself is an act of worship. Every step toward God is a declaration of His worth and our desire for Him.

Jeremiah 29:13 (NIV) "You will seek me and find me when you seek me with all your heart." This promise from God assures us that wholehearted seeking will lead to a deeper understanding of His presence and purpose in our lives.

Application

- Reflect on your personal worship practices. Are you actively seeking God, or have you fallen into the trap of superficial worship? Consider how you can embrace the journey of seeking God with intentionality and sincerity.

- Spend time in prayer, asking God to ignite a passion for His presence and guide you in your pursuit of Him. Commit to seeking Him wholeheartedly, recognizing that true worship requires active engagement and personal devotion.

Challenge Questions

1. How can you ensure that your pursuit of God is sincere and personal, rather than relying on others to seek on your behalf?

2. In what ways can you cultivate a deeper desire for God, allowing it to transform your actions into genuine worship?

3. Reflect on a time when you experienced a meaningful encounter with God. What steps did you take to seek Him, and how can you continue to pursue Him with the same fervor?

By embracing the call to seek God with all our hearts, we align ourselves with His purposes and experience the transformative power of His presence. Let us pursue Him with passion and dedication, recognizing that true worship is a journey of continuous discovery and growth.

Day 29:

The Mind's Eye

Matthew 6:23 (NIV) "Your eyes are like a window for your body. When they are good, you have all the light you need. But when your eyes are bad, everything is dark. If the light inside you is dark, you surely are in the dark."

When I first read this scripture after becoming a Christian, I misunderstood its meaning. I initially thought Jesus was referring to physical eyesight, which made me worried since I wore contact lenses. However, Jesus was not speaking about the natural eyes but rather the eyes of our minds—the mind's eye. In this context, the Greek word used is Ophthalmos, which means the eyes of the mind, the faculty of knowing, and the ability to perceive.

The Fascinating Mind's Eye

The mind's eye is a remarkable concept. Neurologists estimate that the average three-year-old has 1,000,000,000,000,000 (one quadrillion) synaptic connections. These synaptic connections are the links between neurons or between neurons and other types of cells. They are responsible for passing information between neurons, which influences how we perceive the world. The more synaptic connections we have, the greater our ability to perceive and imagine.

Ephesians 1:18 (NIV) "I pray that the eyes of your heart may be enlightened in order that you may know the hope to which he has called you, the riches of his glorious inheritance in his holy people."

This passage highlights the importance of having the eyes of our hearts—our mind's eye—enlightened so that we can understand the hope and calling God has for us. Our ability to imagine and perceive is a gift that allows us to see beyond the natural world.

Imagination vs. Physical Reality

Our ability to imagine things in our mind is far greater than our ability to interpret physical reality. Mathematically speaking, imagination is ten million times more powerful than our five senses combined. This ability to see beyond the tangible is essential to our faith journey.

2 Corinthians 4:18 (NIV) "So we fix our eyes not on what is seen, but on what is unseen, since what is seen is temporary, but what is unseen is eternal." This scripture emphasizes the importance of focusing on the unseen realities of God's kingdom, which are more enduring than the temporary things of this world. Our imagination plays a crucial role in envisioning the promises and truths of God that are not yet visible.

Nurturing the Mind's Eye

Our mind's eye is developed through prayer and nurtured by the Word of God. As Christians, our struggle often lies between two mindsets: Faith and Naturalism. Faith is described in Hebrews 11:1 as being sure of what we hope for and certain of what we do not see. It requires imagination and a belief beyond our five senses.

Romans 10:17 (NIV) "Consequently, faith comes from hearing the message, and the message is heard through the word about Christ."

The Word of God feeds our faith and imagination, enabling us to perceive realities beyond the physical realm. As we engage with Scripture, our mind's eye is opened to the possibilities and promises of God.

The Challenge of Naturalism

Naturalism confines us to the limits of our physical senses. It's the incapacity or reluctance to perceive reality beyond what we can see, touch, hear, smell, or taste. Jesus referred to this as having "bad eyes" full of darkness, indicating an inability to see with the mind's eye.

2 Corinthians 5:7 (NIV) "For we live by faith, not by sight." Living by faith means relying on the unseen truths of God's Word rather than being limited by our sensory perceptions. It challenges us to trust in God's promises even when they are not immediately visible.

Vision Beyond Sight

Helen Keller, who was blind and deaf, once said, "The only thing worse than being blind is having sight but no vision." This profound statement underscores the importance of having a vision beyond physical sight. Our mind's eye allows us to envision a future aligned with God's purposes, inspiring us to move forward in faith.

Proverbs 29:18 (NIV) "Where there is no revelation, people cast off restraint, but blessed is the one who heeds wisdom's instruction."

Vision provides direction and purpose. When we lack vision, we are prone to wander without restraint. But when we cultivate our mind's eye through faith and revelation, we gain clarity and focus on God's calling for our lives.

Application

• Reflect on the state of your mind's eye. Are you nurturing your imagination and faith through prayer and the Word of God, or are you limited by the constraints of naturalism? Consider how you can develop your spiritual vision and align your perception with God's truths.

• Spend time in prayer, asking God to enlighten the eyes of your heart and increase your capacity to see through the lens of faith. Seek His guidance in breaking free from the limitations of physical sight and embracing the fullness of His promises.

Challenge Questions

1.   How can you cultivate a greater awareness of your mind's eye and its role in your faith journey?

2.   In what ways can you shift your focus from naturalism to faith, allowing God's promises to shape your vision and actions?

3.   Reflect on a time when your imagination and faith allowed you to see beyond your circumstances. How did this experience strengthen your relationship with God and influence your actions?

By nurturing our mind's eye through faith and imagination, we align ourselves with God's purposes and open our hearts to the transformative power of His presence. Let us embrace the call to see with spiritual eyes, trusting that God's promises are greater than what we can perceive with our physical senses.

Day 30

Poured from Vessel to Vessel

Jeremiah 48:11 (NIV) "Moab has been at rest from youth, like wine left on its dregs, not poured from one jar to another— she has not gone into exile. So she tastes as she did, and her aroma is unchanged."

The metaphor of being poured from vessel to vessel is powerful in illustrating the process of spiritual growth and transformation. As believers, the concept of being poured is integral to our spiritual journey. This process symbolizes the transitions, trials, and growth necessary to mature in faith and character. The nation of Moab provides a poignant example of what happens when we avoid this refining process: stagnation and an unchanged essence.

The Stagnation of Moab

Moab was a nation known for its pride and political maneuvers. Unlike neighboring nations, Moab had not faced significant conflict or exile, resulting in a sense of complacency. Jeremiah likens Moab to wine left undisturbed on its dregs, illustrating a people unchanged and unchallenged. This metaphor highlights the dangers of spiritual stagnation—without the trials and tribulations that pour us from one vessel to another, we risk becoming static, like Moab, whose taste and aroma remained unchanged.

In spiritual terms, Moab represents individuals or communities who avoid the discomfort of growth and change. Their avoidance of conflict and challenge led to a stagnant state, both culturally and spiritually. They were proud, content in their traditions and idols, and unwilling to undergo the necessary processes to evolve and mature. This serves as a warning to believers: without the process of refinement, we remain unchanged, with a taste and smell that reflects pride and arrogance rather than humility and transformation.

The Necessity of Being Poured

For believers, being poured from vessel to vessel symbolizes the process of spiritual growth and refinement. This involves enduring life's trials and learning from them. It means facing correction, embracing humility, and allowing our motives to be exposed and purified. The process is often uncomfortable and challenging, yet it is essential for developing a robust and mature faith.

Embracing Transitions and Trials

Being poured from vessel to vessel involves navigating transitions and trials. These can be challenging periods, but they are crucial for growth. Transitions often require us to leave behind what is familiar and comfortable, pushing us into new territories of faith and dependence on God. As we embrace these changes, we allow God to shape and mold us according to His purpose.

James 1:2-4 (NIV) "Consider it pure joy, my brothers and sisters, whenever you face trials of many kinds because you know that the testing of your faith produces perseverance. Let perseverance finish its work so that you may be mature and complete, not lacking anything." This passage emphasizes the importance of trials in the maturation process. It encourages believers to embrace challenges with joy, understanding that they lead to spiritual completeness.

Learning from Correction and Exposure

Being poured also involves accepting correction and allowing our hidden motives to be exposed. This process can be uncomfortable as it requires us to confront our weaknesses and areas of sin. However, it is through correction that we grow and become more like Christ.

Hebrews 12:11(NIV) "No discipline seems pleasant at the time, but painful. Later on, however, it produces a harvest of righteousness and peace for those who have been trained by it." Discipline and correction are essential for growth. While they may be painful, they lead to a harvest of righteousness and peace, transforming us into vessels fit for God's use.

Becoming a Sweet-Smelling Offering

The ultimate goal of being poured from vessel to vessel is to become a sweet-smelling offering to the Lord. Like the Apostle Paul, who described himself as a drink offering, we too are called to be poured out in service and sacrifice to God.

> *2 Timothy 4:6-7 (NIV) "For I am already being poured out like a drink offering, and the time for my departure is near. I have fought the good fight, I have finished the race, I have kept the faith."*

Paul's life exemplified the process of being poured out for God's glory. He embraced trials, endured persecution, and ultimately fulfilled his divine purpose. His life serves as an example of what it means to be a vessel refined and ready for God's use.

Application

• Reflect on your own spiritual journey. Are there areas in your life where you have resisted the process of being poured from vessel to vessel? Consider how embracing trials and transitions can lead to greater spiritual maturity and fulfillment of God's purpose.

• Spend time in prayer, asking God to reveal areas where you need to be poured and refined. Seek His guidance in embracing the process of growth and transformation, trusting that He will mold you into a vessel fit for His use.

Challenge Questions

1.   How can you embrace the process of being poured from vessel to vessel in your spiritual journey?

2.   In what ways can you allow God to refine and shape you through trials and transitions?

3.   Reflect on a time when you experienced significant spiritual growth. What role did trials and transitions play in that process?

By embracing the process of being poured from vessel to vessel, we open ourselves to the transformative work of God in our lives. This journey of growth and refinement leads to a deeper, more fulfilling relationship with Him, enabling us to become vessels ready for His purposes. Trust in His process, allowing Him to mold and shape you into a sweet-smelling offering for His glory.

Day 31

You Are One in a Million – An Overcomer!

Romans 8:37 (NIV) "No, in all these things we are more than conquerors through him who loved us."

In fulfilling your purpose, attitude is everything. You've heard it said many times, "Your attitude determines your altitude." Overcoming is an attitude. The ability to win and the capability to overcome is founded simply in our state of being and mindset. Attitude is a state of being which defines our approach, outlook, stance, manner, and position on current situations in life.

Engineered to Win

Your design is not one of defeat; you have been engineered to win. It is in your genes to win battles. You won your biggest battle before you were conceived. While you were still the seed of your biological father, you were the fastest and the strongest. As a sperm, you have the ability to fertilize the egg. You are "one in a million." Before you entered this world, you had been chosen to be a winner. You already have the experience to overcome. You have within your spirit the facility of a champion. Everyone who enters this world has within them the spirit of an overcomer. Understanding this truth gives us the motive to continually adopt the attitude of an overcomer.

Jeremiah 1:5 (NIV) "Before I formed you in the womb, I knew you; before you were born, I set you apart." This verse affirms that God has designed you with purpose and intention. He knows you intimately and has equipped you with the ability to overcome challenges.

Resistance as a Process

Every level of resistance in your life is not an address but a process. Resistance is not a place of permanence but a road to a destination. Resistance comes in the form of challenges, problems, tests, and trials. An overcomer uses the right attitude to overcome. The fact that you have to overcome is evidence that the resistance in your life is a necessary factor in your growth and process. It's designed to increase your capacity so God can trust you with more!

> *James 1:2-4 (NIV) "Consider it pure joy, my brothers and sisters, whenever you face trials of many kinds because you know that the testing of your faith produces perseverance. Let perseverance finish its work so that you may be mature and complete, not lacking anything." Trials are opportunities for growth. Embracing them with a positive attitude helps you to develop perseverance and maturity.*

Choosing to Overcome

Overcoming is not an automatic item; no more than is a prophetic word. Many times, you have to fight; other times, you have to stand, but usually, you just have to believe. Overcoming is a result of a predetermined decision. The fact of the matter is that people simply choose what they want to do. It is in that moment of choice that dreams may be canceled, and purpose deleted. The inability to choose is an ability to handicap one's self.

> *Philippians 4:13 (NIV) "I can do all this through him who gives me strength." This verse reminds us that with God's strength, we can overcome any obstacle. The choice to rely on Him empowers us to triumph over challenges.*

The Mindset of an Overcomer

Be an overcomer today; you are only one thought away from it. God created you as one—why not be one? Overcome, prevail over, triumph over, surmount, and rise above the circumstances that are holding you back. Yo)ur mindset plays a critical role in how you approach life's challenges.

> *2 Timothy 1:7 (NIV) "For God has not given us a spirit of fear, but of power and of love and of a sound mind." God equips us with power, love, and a sound mind. This mindset enables us to face life's difficulties with courage and determination.*

Application

- Reflect on your current attitude toward life's challenges. Are you adopting the mindset of an overcomer, or are you allowing resistance to hold you back? Consider how you can embrace a winning attitude and trust in God's strength to navigate the trials you face.

- Spend time in prayer, asking God to renew your mind and give you the perspective of an overcomer. Seek His guidance in identifying areas where you need to choose victory over defeat.

Challenge Questions

1. How can you cultivate an attitude of overcoming in your daily life?

2. What steps can you take to rely on God's strength and wisdom when facing challenges?

3. Reflect on a past situation where you overcame a difficult circumstance. What mindset and actions contributed to your success?

By embracing the mindset of an overcomer, you align yourself with God's purpose and open yourself to His strength and guidance. Trust in your God-given ability to triumph over life's challenges, knowing that you are one in a million—a conqueror through Christ.

Day 32:

Growing Up vs. Growing Older

Philippians 2:12-13 (NIV) "Continue to work out your salvation with fear and trembling, for it is God who works in you to will and to do of his good purpose."

There is a significant difference between growing older and growing up. Growing older happens naturally, without any effort on our part—it is an involuntary process. However, growing up is a conscious decision that requires intentionality and commitment. While time inevitably ages us, maturity and wisdom are cultivated through deliberate choices and actions.

The Choice to Grow Up

Growing up involves a series of decisions that shape who we are and who we will become. This growth is not automatic; it requires intentionality, often expressed through commitment. Commitment is the daily persistence, diligence, and determination to make choices that lead to maturity—emotionally, spiritually, and intellectually.

1 Corinthians 13:11 "When I was a child, I talked like a child, I thought like a child, I reasoned like a child. When I became a man, I put the ways of childhood behind me." The Apostle Paul highlights the importance of putting away childish ways as we grow into maturity. This process requires more than just the passage of time; it demands a conscious effort to develop wisdom, self-discipline, and a deepened understanding of our purpose in Christ."

The Power of Commitment

Nothing shapes your life more than the commitments you choose to make. Your commitments will either develop you or destroy you, but they will always define you. Consider this: what you are committed to today will determine who you become in the future. If you commit to growth, learning, and the pursuit of God's purpose, your life will reflect those values in the years to come. On the other hand, a lack of commitment will result in stagnation, missed opportunities, and unfulfilled potential.

Matthew 6:33 (NIV) "But seek first his kingdom and his righteousness, and all these things will be given to you as well." Jesus teaches us the importance of prioritizing our commitments—seeking first the kingdom of God ensures that our lives are aligned with His purposes. When we commit to God's priorities, everything else falls into place.

The Consequences of Missed Opportunities

Failures in life are often the result of missed opportunities—opportunities to hear God's voice, to connect with others, to be in the right place at the right time. These missed opportunities are frequently a consequence of not understanding the importance of commitment. Without commitment, we drift through life, disconnected from our purpose, and fail to seize the moments that God has ordained for our growth and success.

Ephesians 5:15-16 (NIV) "See then that you walk circumspectly, not as fools but as wise, redeeming the time, because the days are evil."

Paul's words remind us of the importance of making the most of every opportunity. To "redeem the time" means to live with intentionality, ensuring that we are committed to God's plans and purposes for our lives.

Immaturity vs. Maturity

Choosing not to commit leads to a state of immaturity—growing older in years but remaining immature in attitude and behavior. Maturity, on the other hand, is the result of consistent commitment to growth. It involves making tough decisions, embracing responsibilities, and enduring challenges with perseverance. Immaturity clings to comfort and convenience, while maturity embraces the discomfort of growth and change.

Hebrews 5:14 (NIV) "But solid food is for the mature, who by constant use have trained themselves to distinguish good from evil."

The writer of Hebrews emphasizes that maturity comes from training and practice. It requires a commitment to spiritual growth and a willingness to move beyond the basics of faith.

The Call to Continue

Paul's exhortation in Philippians 2:12-13 is a call to perseverance. He urges us to "continue to work out your salvation with fear and trembling." This continuation is not a one-time effort but a daily commitment to pursue God's will and purpose in our lives. It is a recognition that while God works in us, we also have a responsibility to actively participate in our spiritual growth.

> *Galatians 6:9 (NIV) "Let us not become weary in doing good, for at the proper time we will reap a harvest if we do not give up." This verse encourages us to remain steadfast in our commitments, knowing that persistence will ultimately lead to a fruitful outcome.*

Application and Reflection

Reflect on the commitments you have made in your life. Are they leading you toward growth and maturity, or are they keeping you in a state of immaturity? Consider the areas where you may need to strengthen your commitments to align more closely with God's purposes for your life.

Challenge Questions:

1.   What commitments have you made that are shaping your current life and future?

2.   In what areas of your life do you need to be more intentional about growing up rather than just growing older?

3.   How can you ensure that your commitments are leading you toward spiritual maturity?

4.   What steps can you take today to deepen your commitment to God's purpose for your life?

Growing up is a journey that requires commitment, perseverance, and intentionality. It's time to embrace the call to grow up and not just grow older. Stay connected, remain committed, and watch how God transforms your life as you pursue His purpose with all your heart.

Day 33:

When We Overstay Our Vacation

Rest is a good thing. Very rarely do we find people who have trouble resting from their labor and forward progression in life. Rest is necessary. Rest allows you to recover and replenish for the next season of your life. The Word of God describes rest as a time of reclamation, renovation, recuperation, and refreshing. Resting means being content but never satisfied. The purpose of rest is to keep moving forward.

In Numbers 13-20, God led the nation of Israel to an interesting place, a place of rest and a place of testing. They pushed hard through the wilderness on their way to Canaan, the Promised Land. They arrived at a place called Kadesh. Kadesh was a very large oasis with water flowing underground. It was supposed to be a place of rest that unfortunately turned into a permanent location—the hotel turned into a home! It was there where Moses, in providing the Israelites with water, out of frustration struck the rock with his staff instead of speaking to it as per God's instructions. This mistake cost him entrance into the Promised Land. This should have been a hint for him about overstaying a vacation.

Kadesh, the place of rest, turned into a big problem for Israel; it became the place of setbacks and impediments. Seasons of rest have the potential of becoming seasons of rebellion. The tendency to lose focus is much greater during times of rest.

Major Events at Kadesh

- **Numbers 13-14**

It was the place where ten out of the twelve spies came back with a negative report about entering Canaan. They were afraid of the giants in Canaan and saw themselves as grasshoppers.

- **Numbers 14:39-45**

It was the place where the Israelites sent out an unsanctioned attack against the Amalekites—without God's permission and blessing. They paid for that for centuries!

- **Numbers 20:7-12**

It was the place where Moses was disobedient and struck the rock instead of speaking to the rock to get the people water. That mistake cost him entrance into the Promised Land. He could only see it but never enter it.

- **Numbers 20:1**

It was the place where Miriam, Moses' sister, died—never seeing the Proised Land.

Trouble will always transpire where places of refreshing are turned into permanent places of rest. Remaining too long in our "Kadeshes" will cause us to see our next challenges as impossibilities. We'll begin to see giants instead of opportunities. It's where forcefulness, vision, and work ethic are compromised and an attitude of settling is adopted.

Challenge Questions:

1.   Reflect on a time when you felt stuck in a place of rest. What led you to stay there longer than intended, and how did it affect your spiritual journey?

2.   How can you ensure that your times of rest remain temporary and purposeful, rather than becoming places of stagnation?

3.   What "giants" are you currently facing that may be a result of overstaying your spiritual vacation? How can you shift your perspective to see them as opportunities rather than obstacles?

4.   Take a moment this week to evaluate any area of your life where you might be lingering in a place of rest. Ask God for the strength and courage to move forward into the next phase of your spiritual journey, trusting Him to guide you through the challenges ahead.

Day 34

Exception to the Rule

Lies. I'm researching and studying the lies we believe as Christians. Even though the Word of God specifically clarifies and exposes these lies, we often become predisposed to fall prey to them. On the other hand, the Holy Spirit is the Spirit of Truth. John 16:13 says, "But when He, the Spirit of truth, comes, he will guide you into all truth..." The understanding of this simply implies that when we fall prey to a lie, it's because we aren't permitting lordship to the Holy Spirit and are preventing Him from fully operating in our lives.

> *John 16:13 (NIV) "But when he, the Spirit of truth, comes, he will guide you into all truth. He will not speak on his own; he will speak only what he hears, and he will tell you what is yet to come."*

We all know that bad things occur to people who do badly. But you might say, "Well, not all the time... I know this person...." Yes, for whatever sovereign reason, there seems to be "exceptions to the rule." For example, I know of some people who have smoked for 50 years and are living way past their 70s. But I'm not going to tell my children that it's okay to smoke. There are lottery winners who are wealthy now yet never saved a dime in their lives nor followed Biblical financial principles. Even so, I would not agree that playing the lotto is the best way to plan for your future. It would be asinine to build your life following exceptions to the rule!

> *Proverbs 14:15 (NIV) "The simple believe anything, but the prudent give thought to their steps."*

The truth of the matter is that the exceptions to the rule will always get all the press. They always make the news; people write books about them. Therefore, the enemy wants us to believe that we can be the exception to the rule. There are millions and millions of people who have forfeited their destiny and are now in precarious situations or are in hell because they believed the lie that they could be the "exception to the rule." And to be truthful, usually those who seem to be the exception to the rule in a certain area, somehow at the end of the journey, are by no means the exception to the rule in other areas of life. Being the exception to the rule taxes every other area of your life. NOT worth it—remain PRUDENT!

What Does It Mean to Be Prudent?

Prudence is a virtue that often gets overlooked in today's fast-paced, success-driven society. However, it is a critical aspect of wisdom, deeply rooted in Scripture. To be prudent means to act with care and thought for the future. It's about making decisions that aren't just right for the moment but will also stand the test of time.

The book of Proverbs is filled with references to prudence, often contrasting it with folly. Proverbs 22:3 says, "The prudent see danger and take refuge, but the simple keep going and pay the penalty." This verse highlights that prudence involves foresight and the ability to anticipate consequences. A prudent person recognizes the potential dangers in a course of action and makes adjustments accordingly. They don't just react to situations—they prepare for them.

Prudence is closely related to wisdom and discernment. It's about applying knowledge in a way that is thoughtful and cautious, ensuring that your actions align with God's will. When we exercise prudence, we are more likely to live in a way that honors God and avoids the pitfalls of foolish decisions.

The Dangers of Ignoring Prudence

When we ignore prudence, we often find ourselves taking unnecessary risks or making decisions based on temporary desires or incomplete information. This is where the lie of being the "exception to the rule" becomes dangerous. The enemy wants us to believe that we can bypass the natural consequences of our actions, that somehow, we are different from others who have faced similar situations and failed.

But ignoring prudence doesn't just put us at risk—it can also have a ripple effect on those around us. Our choices impact our families, our communities, and our witness as Christians. By neglecting prudence, we not only jeopardize our own lives but also risk leading others astray.

Galatians 6:7-8 (NIV) reminds us, "Do not be deceived: God cannot be mocked. A man reaps what he sows. Whoever sows to please their flesh, from the flesh will reap destruction; whoever sows to please the Spirit, from the Spirit will reap eternal life." This scripture underscores the importance of prudence in our actions. We must be careful and intentional about what we sow because it will determine what we reap.

Living a Life of Prudence

Living prudently requires a shift in mindset. It means valuing long-term gain over short-term gratification and being willing to make sacrifices now for the sake of future benefits. It's about being proactive rather than reactive, seeking God's wisdom in every decision, and being cautious of the traps that lie in wait for those who disregard His guidance.

Prudent living is not about living in fear or being overly cautious to the point of inaction. Rather, it's about being wise stewards of the resources, time, and opportunities God has given us. It's about recognizing that our lives are not our own and that every decision we make should reflect our commitment to Christ.

James 1:5 (NIV) encourages us, "If any of you lacks wisdom, you should ask God, who gives generously to all without finding fault, and it will be given to you." When we ask God for wisdom, we are seeking the prudence to make decisions that honor Him and lead to a life of integrity and purpose.

Application Questions:

- Have you ever found yourself justifying a behavior or decision because you believed you could be the exception to the rule? What were the outcomes of that decision?

- How can you better recognize the lies that the enemy might be using to convince you that you are the exception?

- What steps can you take to ensure that you are allowing the Holy Spirit to guide you into all truth, especially in areas where you might be tempted to believe otherwise?

- In what areas of your life do you need to exercise more prudence? How can you start making more thoughtful, God-honoring decisions today?

Challenge Questions:

1. Have you ever found yourself justifying a behavior or decision because you believed you could be the exception to the rule? What were the outcomes of that decision?

2. How can you better recognize the lies that the enemy might be using to convince you that you are the exception?

3. What steps can you take to ensure that you are allowing the Holy Spirit to guide you into all truth, especially in areas where you might be tempted to believe otherwise?

4. In what areas of your life do you need to exercise more prudence? How can you start making more thoughtful, God-honoring decisions today?

This week, take a moment to reflect on any areas in your life where you might be living as if you are the exception to the rule. Ask the Holy Spirit to reveal any lies you've believed and to guide you back to the truth. Make a conscious decision to live prudently, trusting that God's principles are for your benefit and His glory.

Day 35

William Tyndale...We Owe It to You!

It's imperative and essential that we become more Biblically aware. As I reflected on this today, I came across a blog by Pastor Mark Batterson that resonated deeply with what was already stirring in my spirit. Pastor Batterson's words are so impactful that I want to share them with you as our first guest blog entry. His message is a timely reminder that we owe a significant debt to William Tyndale—a debt that calls us to appreciate and engage with the Bible in ways that many of us might take for granted.

The Bible We Take for Granted

We live in a time and place where access to the Bible is unparalleled. Many of us have multiple copies, in various translations, easily accessible in our homes. Yet, despite this abundance, we often neglect to read it. This oversight is not just a personal failure; it's a collective one that disconnects us from the sacrifices made by those who came before us—sacrifices that gave us the ability to freely read and study God's Word.

Psalm 119:105 (NIV) "Your word is a lamp for my feet, a light on my path."

William Tyndale: A Life Sacrificed for the Word

William Tyndale was one of the most significant figures in the history of Christianity, yet his name is not as widely recognized as it should be. Tyndale's mission was simple yet profound: he wanted to translate the Bible into English so that every person, regardless of their education or status, could read and understand the Scriptures. His passion for this cause was so intense that it eventually cost him his life.

Tyndale lived during a time when the Bible was only available in Latin, a language that the common person could not read. This meant that the average Christian was entirely dependent on the clergy to interpret the Scriptures for them. Tyndale believed that everyone should have direct access to the Word of God. His famous rebuke to the religious establishment captures his heart: "If

God spare my life, a boy that driveth the plow shall know more of Scripture than thou dost."

The Price of Translation

Tyndale faced immense opposition from the religious authorities of his time. The Bishop of London even ordered that Tyndale's translations be burned. Despite this, Tyndale's resolve only grew stronger. He continued his work in secret, translating the Bible while on the run, fully aware that his efforts could lead to his death.

> *Matthew 5:11-12 (NIV) "Blessed are you when people insult you, persecute you and falsely say all kinds of evil against you because of me. Rejoice and be glad, because great is your reward in heaven, for in the same way they persecuted the prophets who were before you."*

Eventually, Tyndale was captured, charged with heresy, and spent more than a year in a tiny underground prison cell. His captors eventually strangled him to death and burned his body. His final words were a prayer: "Lord, open the King of England's eyes." It was a prayer that God answered. Within a few years, King Henry VIII ordered that an English Bible be placed in every church in Britain. A century later, the King James Version—a translation largely based on Tyndale's work—became one of the most influential books in the English-speaking world.

We Owe It to Tyndale

Tyndale's life and death should serve as a powerful reminder to us all. The Bible we often take for granted was delivered to us through great sacrifice. We owe it to Tyndale—and to all those who have fought to preserve the Scriptures—to read our Bibles, to engage with them, and to allow them to transform our lives. 2 Timothy 3:16-17 (NIV) "All Scripture is God-breathed and is useful for teaching, rebuking, correcting and training in righteousness, so that the servant of God may be thoroughly equipped for every good work."

Your Life as a Translation

While Tyndale translated the Bible into English, you are called to translate the Bible into your life. Your actions, words, and decisions are all translations of the Scriptures that the people around you will read. Many of them may never open a Bible, but they will see its impact through how you live. This reality places a profound responsibility on each of us. We must live in such a way that the truth of God's Word is evident in our lives. Matthew 5:16 (NIV) "In the same way, let your light shine before others, that they may see your good deeds and glorify your Father in heaven."

Application and Reflection

1. Do You Appreciate Your Access to the Bible?
Reflect on how often you read and engage with the Bible. Do you take it for granted? Consider how your approach to the Scriptures might change if you remembered the sacrifices made to give you that access.

2. How Does Your Life Translate the Bible?
Think about the way you live your life. Are your actions a clear and faithful translation of the Scriptures? If not, what changes can you make to better reflect God's Word in your daily life?

3. What Sacrifices Are You Willing to Make for the Gospel?
Tyndale gave his life to ensure that others could read the Bible. What are you willing to do—or give up—to spread the Word of God? Reflect on how you can contribute to the mission of making God's Word known to others.

Challenge Questions

1.   Tyndale was willing to give his life to make God's Word accessible to ordinary people. How does his sacrifice challenge your perspective on the value of Scripture?

2.   Are there areas in your life where you take access to the Bible for granted? How can you cultivate a deeper appreciation for God's Word?

3.   Tyndale faced fierce opposition, yet he remained steadfast in his calling. What obstacles have you faced in your spiritual growth, and how can you stay faithful despite them?

4.   Tyndale's mission was fueled by a desire for people to know truth for themselves. How can you be more intentional in sharing God's Word with others?

This week, make a conscious effort to engage with your Bible daily. Don't just read it—study it, meditate on it, and let it speak into your life. Remember the sacrifices made by those like William Tyndale, and honor them by living out the Word in your everyday actions. Your life is a translation of the Bible that others will read—make sure it's a faithful one.

Day 36:

Principals are Principal

"I keep asking that the God of our Lord Jesus Christ, the glorious Father, may give you the Spirit of wisdom and revelation, so that you may know him better." (Ephesians 1:17)

The Bible is a vast repository of principles, a rich tapestry of truths that undergird our faith and guide our lives. Principles are not merely guidelines; they are essential, underlying rules that define the very fabric of reality as God has ordained it. These principles are foundational truths embedded in our ideologies, values, and doctrines. They are the bedrock upon which successful and righteous living is built.

Understanding the Nature of Principles

Principles are fundamental truths that operate with or without our awareness or consent. Unlike laws that can be broken or ignored, principles remain constant and active, regardless of whether we acknowledge them. They apply themselves naturally to every aspect of life, influencing outcomes and shaping experiences. This is why it is crucial to discover and understand these principles so that we can leverage them for our growth and success.

The fascinating aspect of principles is that they do not require our knowledge to function. For example, the principle of gravity works whether or not we understand the science behind it. Similarly, spiritual principles operate in our lives, often unnoticed, until we begin to uncover their presence through study and revelation.

The Discovery and Application of Principles

The journey of life is, in many ways, a journey of discovery—unearthing the principles that God has woven into the universe and applying them to our lives. Every scientific discovery, every technological innovation, and every advancement in human understanding is rooted in the discovery of principles that were already in place. These discoveries explain patterns that, when understood, reveal practical truths we can apply to our daily lives.

When we discover and apply these principles, we gain wisdom. Wisdom, as the Bible tells us, is the "principal thing." Proverbs 4:7 states, "Wisdom is the principal thing; therefore get wisdom. And in all your getting, get understanding." Here, "principal" means first, beginning, best, chief, and supreme. Wisdom is the foundation upon which all understanding is built. It is through wisdom that we learn to navigate life successfully, making decisions that align with God's will and bring about His desired outcomes.

The Role of the Holy Spirit in Revealing Principles

God's Word is the primary source of principles. Through the Scriptures, we discover the truths that govern life and godliness. However, understanding these principles is not merely an intellectual exercise; it requires the Spirit of wisdom and revelation. As Paul prays in Ephesians 1:17, it is the Holy Spirit who enlightens our minds, enabling us to know God better and to comprehend the principles He has set in motion.

The Holy Spirit, often referred to as the Spirit of Truth, is our guide in this journey of discovery. He opens our eyes to the deeper realities of God's Word, revealing principles that transform our belief system and align it with God's truth. This transformation is ongoing; as we grow in our relationship with God, we continually uncover new principles that shape our understanding and behavior.

The Power of Principles in Shaping Our Lives

The application of principles is what we call wisdom, and wisdom is crucial for living a life that pleases God and fulfills His purposes for us. Principles are like the roots of a tree; they ground us, give us stability, and enable us to grow and bear fruit. When we ignore principles, we find ourselves struggling, much like a tree with shallow roots in a storm. However, when we discover and apply these principles, we find ourselves living in alignment with God's design, experiencing peace, joy, and success.

For instance, the principle of sowing and reaping is one that operates in every area of life. Galatians 6:7 says, "Do not be deceived: God cannot be mocked. A man reaps what he sows." This principle applies to our relationships, our work, our finances, and our spiritual growth. When we sow kindness, we reap kindness. When we invest in our relationship with God, we reap spiritual growth and deeper intimacy with Him.

A Call to Pursue Wisdom

The pursuit of wisdom is a lifelong journey. It requires a hunger for understanding and a deep desire to know God more intimately. As we draw closer to Him, the Holy Spirit reveals the principles that will guide us into all truth. This journey is not about acquiring knowledge for the sake of knowledge but about transforming our lives to reflect the character and purposes of God.

As believers, we must be intentional in our pursuit of wisdom. This means committing ourselves to the study of God's Word, seeking the guidance of the Holy Spirit, and applying the principles we discover in our daily lives. It is through this process that we grow in maturity and are equipped to fulfill the purpose for which God created us.

Application and Reflection

1. Are You Aware of the Principles Governing Your Life?
Reflect on the principles you live by. Are they aligned with God's Word? Consider how these principles have shaped your decisions, relationships, and growth.

2. How Are You Pursuing Wisdom?
Think about your daily practices. Are you intentional in your pursuit of wisdom? How can you deepen your study of the Scriptures and your reliance on the Holy Spirit for guidance?

3. Are You Applying What You Learn?
It's not enough to discover principles; we must also apply them. Reflect on how well you apply the principles you've learned. Are there areas in your life where you struggle to put wisdom into practice?

Challenge Questions

1. Are You Aware of the Principles Governing Your Life?
Reflect on the principles you live by. Are they aligned with God's
Word? Consider how these principles have shaped your decisions,
relationships, and growth.

2. How Are You Pursuing Wisdom? Think about your daily
practices. Are you intentional in your pursuit of wisdom? How can
you deepen your study of the Scriptures and your reliance on the
Holy Spirit for guidance?

3. Are You Applying What You Learn? It's not enough to
discover principles; we must also apply them. Reflect on how well you
apply the principles you've learned. Are there areas in your life where
you struggle to put wisdom into practice?

This week, commit to discovering and applying at least one new principle from
God's Word. Allow the Holy Spirit to guide you into all truth and transform
your understanding. As you do, watch how God's wisdom begins to shape your
life, leading you into greater alignment with His will and purpose.

Day 37:

How God Rewards

Matthew 25:23 (NIV) "His master replied, 'Well done, good and faithful servant! You have been faithful with a few things; I will put you in charge of many things. Come and share your master's happiness!'"

The Gift and Responsibility of Life

Galatians 6:7 (NIV) "Do not be deceived: God cannot be mocked. A man reaps what he sows." Life is a gift. Life is a privilege. And how we manage that gift will determine what we'll receive within it. Life's rewards from God only come through the ambit of proper management. How we manage life itself will determine whether we'll receive rewards and promotions within it. Rewards and promotions in life are dictated by the way we steward life in general. God will not be mocked...we will reap what we sow.

Life is not simply about existing; it's about managing the gifts and opportunities God has entrusted to us. Our rewards, both in this life and in the life to come, are directly tied to how well we steward what we have been given.

The Fallacy of Entitlement

Romans 6:23 (NIV) "For the wages of sin is death, but the gift of God is eternal life in Christ Jesus our Lord." Unfortunately, most people live their lives thinking that life itself owes them something. The reality is that the only thing we deserve is HELL. Thank God for His grace and mercy! But we need to understand that though God loves us by His grace, He won't reward nor promote us because of His grace. The fact is that rewards are NOT a matter of His grace but our works. Remember, we will always give an account for what we do and don't do. And we will reap in this life and the next according to the way we manage our lives now. In the Kingdom of God, there is no such thing as a social promotion. It's all about management.

Grace is the foundation of our salvation, but it is not the basis for our rewards. God's rewards are connected to our actions, our obedience, and our stewardship. Living with a sense of entitlement blinds us to the truth that God's blessings and promotions are a result of faithful service and good management of what He has entrusted to us.

Stewardship and Accountability

> *2 Corinthians 5:10 (NIV) "For we must all appear before the judgment seat of Christ, so that each of us may receive what is due us for the things done while in the body, whether good or bad."*

The concept of stewardship is central to understanding how God rewards us. Stewardship is the responsible management of resources, talents, time, and opportunities that God has given us. Our faithfulness in these areas is what determines our rewards. God's system is not based on favoritism but on faithfulness.

The parable of the talents in Matthew 25 serves as a reminder that our rewards are directly tied to how well we manage what we have been given. The servant who was faithful with little was given much more, while the servant who was unfaithful lost even what he had. This principle applies to every aspect of our lives.

Practical Application:

• Reflect on how you are managing the resources, talents, and opportunities God has given you. Identify areas where you can improve your stewardship and align more closely with God's expectations.

• Develop a plan for being more intentional in your actions, ensuring that you are living in a way that honors God and positions you for His rewards.

Application

> *1 Corinthians 3:13-14 (NIV) "Their work will be shown for what it is, because the Day will bring it to light. It will be revealed with fire, and the fire will test the quality of each person's work. If what has been built survives, the builder will receive a reward."*

Reflect on how you can actively improve your stewardship, ensuring that your actions align with God's expectations and position you for His rewards. Consider how you can be more intentional in your daily life, focusing on faithfulness and obedience.

Challenge Questions

1.   In what areas of your life do you need to improve your stewardship, ensuring that you are managing the resources, talents, and opportunities God has entrusted to you?
Reflect on your current habits and practices, identifying areas where you can be more faithful in your stewardship.

2.   How can you develop a plan for being more intentional in your actions, ensuring that you are living in a way that honors God and positions you for His rewards?
Identify practical steps to align your daily decisions and actions with God's principles of stewardship and accountability.

3.   What steps can you take to ensure that your actions and decisions are guided by a desire to please God and receive His rewards, rather than by a sense of entitlement?
Consider how you can cultivate a mindset of humility and faithfulness, recognizing that rewards come through obedience and good management.

Understanding how God rewards us is essential for living a life that is pleasing to Him and fulfilling our purpose. By focusing on stewardship, accountability, and faithful service, we position ourselves to receive the rewards and promotions that God desires to give us. Let us strive to manage our lives well, ensuring that our actions reflect His love and purpose in all we do.

Day 38

Choose Your Road

Proverbs 14:12 (NIV) "There is a way that appears to be right, but in the end it leads to death."

The Deceptive Quest for Happiness

Jeremiah 17:9 (NIV) "The heart is deceitful above all things and beyond cure. Who can understand it?"

Why do seemingly smart people make choices they end up regretting later on? As you read the biographies of individuals who are obviously highly educated and, therefore, in principle, exceptionally intelligent, they all have made decisions that took them down a road they didn't want to be on. For the record, you don't have to be uneducated to find yourself "in a pickle." Problems, issues, troubles, and tribulations occur to all of us regardless of our culture, upbringing, and education. And just about all of them were our very own choice—but why?!

Our problem rarely stems from a lack of education or instruction. It's not a deficiency in information we have but rather an inability to pursue the truth. Unfortunately, we don't wake up every morning desiring and longing to know what is true, genuine, and sincere. By default, our human nature, regardless of its intellect, isn't on a truth quest but rather on a happiness quest! We desire to feel happy; therefore, we make decisions that lead to making us feel "happy." Usually, our pursuit of happiness overrides the sacrificial choice of reason and conviction that places us on the pathway of integrity, character, nobleness, and truth.

The Soul's Deception vs. the Spirit's Conviction

Romans 8:6 (NIV) "The mind governed by the flesh is death, but the mind governed by the Spirit is life and peace."

Don't get me wrong; there is nothing wrong with wanting to be happy. The problem is that certain choices are made from the soul rather than the spirit. The soul is deceptive—it usually desires what makes it feel good for that moment. It bypasses logic and intellect, and it certainly bypasses the conscience—the conviction of the Holy Spirit.

Have you ever bought something you regretted later on? I'm not just talking about clothes in the mall, but cars, houses, jewelry, etc. Have you ever eaten something you know you should not have? Have you ever been in a relationship with someone that you now regret for the rest of your life? This explains why people end up in rehab centers with life-controlling vices and why we have so many unwed mothers out there. The pursuit of happiness is founded on a desire to feel good, but the pursuit of truth is founded not by feelings or desires, but by a conviction to know the voice of the Holy Spirit. There is nothing wrong with wanting to be happy, but the happiness must be based on truth and character, not lusts and covetousness. Every day and every waking minute, we must choose which road to take—the road of happiness or the road of truth.

The Road Less Traveled: Pursuing Truth

> *John 16:13 (NIV) "But when he, the Spirit of truth, comes, he will guide you into all the truth."*

True happiness is found not in the fleeting satisfaction of temporary pleasures but in the lasting joy that comes from living in alignment with God's truth. When we choose the road of truth, we may face challenges and sacrifices, but we also experience the deep peace and fulfillment that comes from living according to God's will.

The pursuit of truth is a deliberate choice to listen to the Holy Spirit's guidance, even when it contradicts our immediate desires. It requires us to evaluate our motives, seek God's wisdom, and trust that His path, though it may be narrow, leads to life and true joy.

Practical Application:

- **Reflect on the decisions you have made recently and assess whether they were driven by a pursuit of happiness or a pursuit of truth.**

- **Ask the Holy Spirit to help you discern the motives behind your choices, guiding you to make decisions that are rooted in truth and aligned with God's will.**

Application

Psalm 119:105 (NIV) "Your word is a lamp for my feet, a light on my path."

Reflect on how you can actively pursue truth in your decision-making, ensuring that your choices are guided by the Holy Spirit and aligned with God's will. Consider how you can resist the temptation to pursue fleeting happiness and instead focus on the enduring joy that comes from walking in truth.

Challenge Questions

1. In what areas of your life do you find yourself tempted to pursue happiness at the expense of truth, and how can you realign your decisions with God's will?
Reflect on your current decision-making process and identify areas where you can prioritize truth over temporary satisfaction.

2. How can you develop a deeper sensitivity to the Holy Spirit's guidance, ensuring that your choices are rooted in integrity and aligned with God's truth?
Identify practical steps to cultivate a closer relationship with the Holy Spirit, seeking His guidance in all aspects of your life.

3. What steps can you take to ensure that your pursuit of happiness is grounded in truth and character, leading to lasting joy and fulfillment?

Choosing the right road is essential for living a life that is pleasing to God and fulfilling His purpose. By focusing on the pursuit of truth rather than temporary happiness, we position ourselves to experience lasting joy and fulfillment. Let us strive to make decisions that are guided by the Holy Spirit and aligned with God's will, ensuring that our lives reflect His truth and love in all we do.

Day 39:

Breakthrough Attitude

2 Corinthians 4:8-9 (NIV) "We are hard pressed on every side, but not crushed; perplexed, but not in despair; persecuted, but not abandoned; struck down, but not destroyed."

The Power of Attitude

Proverbs 23:7 (NKJV) "For as he thinks in his heart, so is he."

Attitudes are not innate; they are developed. Attitudes are formed by the choices we make within the conditions we experience. Life has a way, to many people, of forming attitudes in the same way a river shapes the topography of a region. How we handle the rivers of life will determine our stance in life. We were designed to experience breakthroughs and not breakdowns. God engineered us to manifest miracles by aligning ourselves with Him. Breakthroughs should be a constant staple of our diet of achievement. And it's all in our attitude!

Attitude is a powerful force that shapes our responses to life's challenges. It determines whether we see obstacles as insurmountable barriers or as opportunities for growth and victory. A breakthrough attitude is not just about positive thinking; it's about aligning our thoughts, beliefs, and actions with God's truth and promises.

Four Characteristics of a Breakthrough Attitude

Philippians 4:13 (NIV) "I can do all this through him who gives me strength."

1.   A Breakthrough Attitude Rejects Rejection

Romans 8:37 (NIV) "No, in all these things we are more than conquerors through him who loved us."

A breakthrough attitude refuses to be rejected, keeps coming back, and continues to show up for battle. It can't be discouraged or disqualified. It refuses to be offended and will never become bitter. This kind of attitude understands that rejection is not the end of the story but a stepping stone to greater things.

It's about perseverance and resilience, knowing that God's approval is the only validation that truly matters.

2. A Breakthrough Attitude Sees Setbacks as Temporary

James 1:2-3 (NIV) - "Consider it pure joy, my brothers and sisters, whenever you face trials of many kinds, because you know that the testing of your faith produces perseverance."

Every temporary setback is nothing more than a stage for a major comeback. President Harry S. Truman in 1922, at the age of 38, was in debt and unemployed, but in 1945 he became the most powerful leader in the free world. If he had seen his setback as permanent, he wouldn't have ever fulfilled his purpose. A breakthrough attitude sees beyond the current difficulties and envisions the victory ahead. It's about trusting God's timing and believing that He is working all things together for our good.

3. A Breakthrough Attitude Focuses on Strengths

Philippians 4:8 (NIV) "Finally, brothers and sisters, whatever is true, whatever is noble, whatever is right, whatever is pure, whatever is lovely, whatever is admirable— if anything is excellent or praiseworthy—think about such things."

What distinguishes winners from losers is that winners develop an ability to concentrate on what they're able to do instead of what they're unable to do. A breakthrough attitude focuses on strengths, not weaknesses. It identifies the gifts and abilities God has given and leverages them for His glory. This attitude cultivates gratitude and optimism, recognizing that God has equipped us with everything we need to succeed in His purpose.

4. A Breakthrough Attitude Bounces Back

Micah 7:8 (NIV) "Do not gloat over me, my enemy! Though I have fallen, I will rise. Though I sit in darkness, the Lord will be my light."

A breakthrough attitude is resilient. It has the ability to bounce back from adversity. The Apostle Paul said it best: "We are hard pressed on every side, but not crushed; perplexed, but not in despair; persecuted, but not abandoned; struck down, but not destroyed." This kind of attitude refuses to stay down after a fall. It recognizes that setbacks are not final and that God's strength is made perfect in our weakness. Resilience is the hallmark of a breakthrough attitude, enabling us to rise again and continue the fight.

Application

> *Hebrews 12:1-2 (NIV) "Therefore, since we are surrounded by such a great cloud of witnesses, let us throw off everything that hinders and the sin that so easily entangles. And let us run with perseverance the race marked out for us, fixing our eyes on Jesus, the pioneer and perfecter of faith."*

Reflect on the characteristics of a breakthrough attitude and identify areas where you may need to shift your mindset. Ask God to help you develop resilience, focus on your strengths, and see setbacks as opportunities for growth. Consider how you can cultivate an attitude that rejects rejection and continually seeks God's truth and promises.

Challenge Questions

1.   In what areas of your life do you struggle with rejection, and how can you develop an attitude that refuses to be discouraged or disqualified?
Reflect on how you can anchor your identity in Christ and His love, allowing His approval to guide your responses to rejection.

2.   How can you begin to view your current setbacks as temporary stages for a major comeback?
Consider how you can trust God's timing and remain hopeful, even in the face of difficulties.

3.   What steps can you take to focus more on your strengths and the gifts God has given you, rather than dwelling on your weaknesses?
Identify practical ways to cultivate gratitude and leverage your strengths for God's glory.

A breakthrough attitude is essential for experiencing the victories and miracles God has in store for us. By cultivating resilience, focusing on strengths, rejecting rejection, and viewing setbacks as temporary, we align ourselves with God's purpose and position ourselves for breakthroughs. Let us strive to develop an attitude that reflects God's truth and His unwavering promises, enabling us to overcome every challenge and achieve the success He desires for our lives.

Day 40:

Fewer Efforts, Greater Results

We have heard it said, "less is more." This principle is true in many ways. It's a 19th-century proverbial phrase that references the paradigm of simplicity and focus. It is often associated with the architect and furniture designer Ludwig Mies Van Der Rohe, one of the founders of modern architecture and a proponent of simplicity of style. He is responsible for much of the inspiration behind modern architecture. He had a candid ability to design and create multi-functional structures and furniture, aesthetic to the eye, with minimal resources and effort.

I believe that is how the Lord wants us to follow Him. We have a propensity to greatly complicate things. The direct result of prayer is simplicity and focus. When we begin to understand the heart of God, less will always be more. When we endeavor to undertake a directive from the Lord without a constant pursuit of purpose in prayer, it will always result in greater effort on our part. The consequences are usually wasted resources and valuable time (been there, done that, and got no T-shirt). With prayer as a focus, there will always be fewer efforts and greater results.

> *Zechariah 4:6 (NIV) "So he said to me, 'This is the word of the LORD to Zerubbabel: 'Not by might nor by power, but by my Spirit,' says the LORD Almighty.'"*

> *Philippians 4:13 (NIV) "I can do all this through him who gives me strength."*

The Principle of "Less is More"

In the Kingdom of God, the principle of "less is more" is profoundly evident. When we align our actions with God's will through prayer, we experience His power working through us, leading to more effective results with less effort. Our tendency to complicate matters is replaced by divine simplicity, where God's plans are clear and achievable.

Simplicity in Action

The architect Ludwig Mies Van Der Rohe demonstrated the power of simplicity in his designs. His ability to create functional and beautiful structures with minimal resources serves as a metaphor for how we can live our lives. By focusing on what truly matters and eliminating unnecessary complexities, we can achieve more with less effort.

Prayer as a Focus

When prayer is at the center of our lives, it brings clarity and direction. Prayer helps us align our desires with God's will, reducing the energy wasted on fruitless endeavors. It allows us to tap into the divine power that multiplies our efforts and magnifies our results.

Practical Application

- **Set Clear Goals:** Simplify your objectives by seeking God's guidance through prayer. Focus on what He has called you to do, rather than being distracted by every opportunity.

- **Trust in God's Strength:** Rely on the Holy Spirit to empower your actions. As Zechariah 4:6 reminds us, success comes not by human might or power but by God's Spirit.

- **Celebrate Simplicity:** Embrace the concept of "less is more" in your daily life. By focusing on fewer tasks and doing them well, you allow God to bring about greater results.

The Power of Alignment

When our efforts are aligned with God's purposes, we witness the miraculous unfolding of His plans. Instead of striving in our strength, we become vessels for His work. The Holy Spirit empowers us to accomplish what seems impossible, turning our modest efforts into significant outcomes.

The Role of Prayer

Prayer is the key to alignment with God's will. It tunes our hearts to His desires and opens the door for His power to work through us. As we seek Him, we gain the wisdom and insight needed to navigate life's challenges effectively.

Maximizing Impact

In our 10,000 Doors project, we have witnessed the power of simplicity and prayer. We trust that He will maximize our impact by focusing our efforts on sharing God's love with our community. This project is not about numbers but about reaching hearts and changing lives.

Challenge Questions

1.   How can you incorporate the principle of "less is more" into your daily life and ministry?

2.   In what areas do you need to rely more on God's Spirit rather than your strength and effort?

3.   Reflect on a time when prayer simplified a complex situation for you. How did it change your approach and results?

The principle of "less is more" teaches us that God's ways are higher than ours. When we surrender our plans and align ourselves with His will, we experience His power working through us. Let us embrace simplicity and focus, trusting that God will achieve greater results through our lives as we depend on Him. With prayer as our guide, we can accomplish more with less, knowing that His Spirit empowers us for every task He calls us to undertake.

Conclusion

Reflections on the Journey

As we come to the close of this 40-day journey of spiritual growth, it's essential to pause and reflect on the transformation that has taken place within us. This journey has been more than just a series of daily readings; it has been a profound pilgrimage into the depths of our faith, a time of intentional focus on becoming the people God has called us to be.

Throughout these days, we have explored various aspects of our spiritual lives—attitudes that lead to breakthroughs, the power of consistency, the importance of commitment, and the necessity of overcoming obstacles with a steadfast spirit. Each lesson was not just a step forward in knowledge but a deliberate move towards a deeper understanding of God's purpose for our lives.

We've learned that spiritual growth is not a passive process. It requires active engagement, a willingness to be shaped and molded by God's hand. We've embraced the idea that growing up in our faith is a choice, not just a natural byproduct of growing older. This journey has taught us that we are not just hearers of the Word but doers—actively applying the principles we've learned to our daily lives.

As we reflect on these past 40 days, we can see that every challenge we faced was an opportunity to deepen our faith. Every lesson learned was a building block in our spiritual foundation. We've discovered that setbacks are not permanent but are stepping stones to greater heights in our spiritual walk. We've realized that God's rewards and promotions come through our diligent stewardship of the life He has given us.

This journey has also reminded us of the importance of unity and teamwork within the body of Christ. We've understood that we are not on this journey alone but are part of a greater community, each of us contributing our unique gifts and strengths to the whole. Together, we've learned to stand firm in our faith, to face persecution and trials with courage, and to support one another in love.

Now, as we stand at the end of this 40-day journey, it is not merely an end but a beginning. The seeds of spiritual growth that have been planted in our hearts over these days are just the start of a lifelong pursuit of God's presence and purpose. The lessons we've learned are not to be forgotten but to be lived out daily, becoming the foundation of a life that reflects Christ in every way.

Let us move forward with renewed passion and a breakthrough attitude that refuses to settle for anything less than God's best. Let us continue to seek Him with all our hearts, knowing that He is faithful to complete the good work He has started in us. As we apply what we've learned, we will see the fruit of this journey—a life that is continually growing, maturing, and bearing witness to the transformative power of God.

Remember, this is not just the end of a 40-day journey; it is the beginning of a new chapter in your walk with Christ. Embrace it fully, and watch as God continues to lead you from glory to glory. Your journey of spiritual growth is far from over—it's only just begun.

About The Author

Manny Rivera, alongside his wife Victoria, has been a transformative leader in ministry for over three decades. Together with their spiritual sons and daughters, they have planted three thriving churches and traveled across the globe, speaking at conferences and training leaders in both ministry and marketplace settings. Manny current- ly oversees these three churches and serves as the Lead Pastor of Discover Life Church in Lawrenceville, Georgia, where his impact continues to ripple through the lives of his congregation and beyond.

Manny's ministry journey began in an unexpected place—a promising career in baseball. However, a life-altering encounter with Jesus radically changed his trajectory, compelling him to step away from baseball and into full-time minis- try. Since then, Manny has been driven by a singular passion: to ignite spiritual revival and raise up the next generation of leaders who will carry the fire of the Gospel.

For over 34 years, Manny has devoted himself to training ministry and business leaders through his Timothy Team, a unique discipleship program designed for those seeking to fulfill God's call on their lives. A relentless pursuit of revival, discipleship, and kingdom advancement fuels his leadership. Known for his raw, unfiltered preaching style, Manny's messages are infused with the power of the Holy Spirit, consistently challenging people to live with conviction, purpose, and a deep connection to Christ.

Manny and Victoria are proud parents to four amazing adult children—Calysta, Zayne, Zion (married to Erika), and Zealynd—who continue to inspire them in their walk with God. Manny finds peace and rejuvenation in nature outside of ministry, often hiking and discovering new trails. His love for travel allows him to engage with diverse cultures and bring the message of Christ to the nations, whether he's speaking at international conferences or building relationships across the world.

www.ingramcontent.com/pod-product-compliance
Lightning Source LLC
Chambersburg PA
CBHW060927120626
46557CB00003B/901